# HOW TO RIDE WELL

by

JOSEPHINE
PULLEIN-THOMPSON

CAVALIER PAPERBACKS

This revised edition published by Cavalier Paperbacks
1996

Burnham House
Jarvis St
Upavon
Wilts SN9 6DU

Cover Design Nancy Lawrence



ISBN 1-899470-30-1

Printed and bound by Cox and Wyman, Reading, Berks

# CONTENTS

# CHAPTER ONE

## HOW TO BEGIN

In the days before McAdam and Telford turned the muddy and deeply rutted turnpikes of England into hard roads, there were only two certain ways of getting from place to place, you walked or you rode. Almost everyone learned to ride just as nowadays almost everyone can bicycle or drive a car, but, because to most of them the horse was just a form of transport, few of them bothered to ride well; so long as they could stay on they were quite content.

Now the position is entirely different, horses are rarely used as transport in fact they themselves are transported about in horse-boxes, trailers and planes; riding has stopped being essential or even useful and has become a pleasure and, because enjoyment is now the whole point of riding, the mere ability to stay on isn't going to content us for long.

Everyone has known the misery of doing something badly, if you ride badly this feeling is doubled because the pony is miserable too and, in the same way, your pleasure is increased when things go well for you always have someone to share your excitements and triumphs.

There are people who think it sporting to perform badly and to enter for competitions in which one doesn't stand a chance, 'to have a bash'. But in riding this frequently means that the horse does actually get bashed in some way. He may bang or bruise his legs jumping jumps that are too high for him or have his mouth terribly hurt because the jumps are too high for his rider; he may damage his lungs if he is galloped too far for his state of fitness.

Once you are mounted there are two people to be considered, you and your pony, and you should both enjoy yourselves. There are few more dreary sights than a pony and rider perpetually at loggerheads and few more poetic ones than a pony and rider in complete harmony. It is in the achieving of this harmony that the greatest pleasures of riding are to be found; in the building of a partnership in which you can act as one, without effort or argument, and with only the slightest of signals, but this is only possible if you learn to ride well.

### *Beginners' ponies*

Buying a pony is not the best way to learn to ride unless you have someone in your family who knows a good deal about ponies, is willing to teach you and has the time to take you out riding nearly every day.

When you start riding you are called a beginner and

very few ponies can stand being handled entirely by a beginner. They are irritated by inexperienced and fumbling hands, dragging bridles over their eyes and banging bits against their teeth. They become angry or apprehensive about being saddled when they've been pinched by the girth and about being mounted when the rider's toe has dug into their stomachs; gradually they become bad-tempered or nervous or headstrong according to their characters. On the other hand, you can't learn to saddle, bridle or mount without practising, but don't expect any pony to stand too much of it at a time.

Teaching yourself to ride is a long, slow and disheartening way of learning, don't believe people who tell you that riding is just a matter of practice, in fact the more you practise with an incorrect seat or a faulty leg position the harder it will be to shed this habit later.

You must be taught: you must learn the proper way to sit, to hold the reins and to give the aids and it is only when you've learned this much, that practice by itself can improve you. As you become more experienced you will observe for yourself, that it is possible to ride for twenty years and still be a thoroughly bad rider; a state of affairs which you want to avoid.

Another disadvantage of buying a pony before you can ride is that it will have to be a very quiet, slow, stolid sort of pony which ignores all but the most obvious aids. As you learn, this sort of pony will become rather dull to ride. What were virtues when you were green and nervous will become faults when you are confident and, after a time, your riding will stop improving, simply because you will have learned all you can from this type of pony. You will then be faced with the misery of parting from a friend, or, if you decide to keep him, of losing all hope of increasing your skill as a rider.

This last situation is a very depressing one and many people who give up riding after a few years do so because they never had the chance of acquiring a second pony with more exciting possibilities. If you have younger brothers and sisters the position is quite different. They will be eager to take over from you and, when you graduate to a larger and more difficult mount, you will still be able to ride the original pony occasionally to prevent him getting out of hand as ponies do if they are ridden only by beginners. But you, as the first rider in the family, will need at least twelve lessons before the pony is bought.

### *Leading rein ponies*

Parents of very young beginners sometimes buy ponies on which to lead them out. Elderly, semi-retired ponies capable of only light work are best for this job, but if a young or middle-aged pony is bought, arrangements should be made for an older and more experienced child to ride him fairly regularly, this will prevent him becoming fat and bored or over-fresh and badly behaved according to his disposition.

Pony Club secretaries can often put parents in touch with lightweight riders who ride as often as they can afford at riding-schools, but cannot have ponies of their own. A rider of about twelve who is C test standard should be capable of exercising any normal small pony and of taking it to rallies and gymkhanas without doing it any harm.

*Riding schools*

Probably the best way to learn to ride, if no one in your family knows much about horses, is to take lessons at a local riding-school. If it is a good riding-school it will take you under its wing and, later on, it will help you to buy your pony and advise you about saddlery and feeding problems. Also, as it will have staff capable of instructing to an advanced level, you will be able to go on learning, taking a weekly lesson on your own pony, long after you have passed the beginner stage.

Unfortunately, it is extremely difficult to make a living at teaching riding so there are not a great many good schools about and the price of lessons at the first-class establishments is more than many parents can afford. There are, however, some very good small schools run by people who love horses, have a vocation for teaching and are content to remain poor.

This kind of riding-school is generally short of staff and the pupils are encouraged to help with the grooming, tack-cleaning and general care of the ponies. This is a great advantage, for even if you have no hope of owning a pony, the handling of them makes you a better and more sympathetic rider and people who know how to look after them are always in demand; when you are experienced you will frequently find yourself acting as temporary owner while your friends are on holiday and in this way you will have a great deal of riding and fun and become very experienced at managing different types of pony.

*Bad riding schools*

Riding schools where the ponies are obviously underfed, over-worked - all ponies need one day of rest each week - or where the saddlery doesn't fit should be avoided as there is no pleasure in riding a pony that is tired out, weak with hunger or in pain from a badly-fitting saddle. Fortunately this type of school is rare now that all riding schools must be inspected and licensed.

The most usual type of school is one where the ponies are fed and cared for but they are not particularly well-schooled, that is trained, and the instruction of the riders is vague or sometimes actually wrong.

If a riding school has nowhere to give proper lessons: no paddock, no marked out menage or school, you are not going to learn very much there. Going out for rides or 'hacking' will teach you to walk, trot and canter and to stay on, but it will never make you into a good rider. If this is the only type of riding school in the area where you live, learn all you can there then buy a pony of your own and continue to learn from books and the Pony Club.

*Learning from friends*

There are two streams of knowledge which you pass on when you are teaching: one is all that you have been taught and the other is what you learned from your own thought and experience. A friend of your own age, or a few years older, will not have had much time to gather experience so the important thing to discover, before you begin to absorb everything that he or she tells you is by whom was he or she instructed. Sometimes a teenager who has graduated to a larger mount keeps an outgrown pony and takes a few pupils to pay for his keep. If the teenager has been well-taught and is able to pass on knowledge this can be a very good way of learning to ride.

Entirely self-taught people should be avoided as they are just as likely to pass on their faults as their good points. And, remember, that while winning gymkhana events is not necessarily a sign of being a good rider, much less a good instructor, anyone who has passed Pony Club test B should have acquired a certain amount of sensible information.

*Learning from the Pony Club*

Once you are able to walk, trot and canter you can learn a great deal by joining the Pony Club and going to rallies. You can also make friends, enjoy pony-less parties and outings and get advice about everything connected with ponies and riding from the officials and instructors. What the Pony Club can't teach you is the very elementary part of riding because complete beginners need to be on the leading rein or in an enclosed space with not more than two or three to an instructor. Also a lesson once a week is the absolute minimum when you start learning to ride, you will progress more than twice as fast if you have two lessons each week in the beginning. Few Pony Club branches provide that number of working rallies.

If you are being taught by one of your parents, the Pony Club can be of great help as parents who learned to ride when they were young sometimes grow old fashioned, while the Pony Club instructors are kept up to date by conferences and courses.

If you are unable to have a pony of your own you can still join the Pony Club and go to all the functions, hiring a pony from a riding-school for the mounted rallies when you can afford it.

*What to wear*

Having found someone to teach you to ride you must now dress for the part.The essential clothes are a hard hat, jodhpurs and boots or a pair of stout leather shoes.

Hard hats are compulsory wear for Pony Club rallies and for jumping competitions held under BSJA rules and sensible riders wear them for hacking as well. If you have a fall they save your head from being cut by stones or kicked by hoofs and they also soften the impact with which it meets the ground. Not all hard hats are efficient so make sure you buy one of a brand that has been tested by the British Standards Institution and has their kite mark inside, or one that has been approved by the European Union. As you become more adventurous and especially if you take up cross-country riding, you should graduate to a jockey skull cap.

Jodhpurs or breeches are essential if you want to ride well. Jeans will do for just sitting on a pony or for riding bareback, but for serious riding they are too inclined to work up the rider's legs or to go into wrinkles on the inside of the knee. They make sitting with the correct seat uncomfortable and so encourage bad riding.

The right sort of boot or shoe is important because accidents are often caused by flimsy shoes with no heel slipping right through the stirrups or by wellies jamming in them. If a rider falls with one foot caught in a stirrup he may be dragged which is a very unnerving experience, so never ride in sandals, trainers, wellies or flimsy feminine shoes.

A riding coat isn't necessary until you begin to compete in shows; a shirt, sweater or anorak will do quite well until then. But if you do buy a coat, buy a tweed one and not a black or dark blue coat as they ought only to be worn at very formal horse occasions and with breeches and black boots, not with jodhpurs; they are definitely incorrect wear for Pony Club rallies. Girls should avoid frilly shirts and jewellery and dress to look dashing rather than feminine.

A pair of string gloves are an important possession if

there is any chance of you riding in the rain as they stop the wet reins sliding through your hands and, after your first few lessons, you should acquire and get into the habit of riding with a small light whip; it is far better to give a lazy pony a tap with a whip than to be perpetually kicking him.

## CHAPTER TWO

## FIRST LESSONS

Always introduce yourself to a pony before you mount. Walk up to him from the front or from the side and say, "Hello, how are you?" or something like that. Pat him on the neck, don't stroke his nose as most ponies hate this. Try to talk to him in your ordinary voice - the one in which you talk to your friends when you are in a good temper. Ponies judge you much more by the tone of your voice than by the words you use and if you sound nervous or frightened or angry they will be influenced by that no matter what soothing words you are saying. Try to be natural; ponies see through people who put on a noisy, hearty, over-confident manner, but on the other hand they don't like being addressed in a mousy whisper and they hate whiners. Some people who have never had a dog or a cat feel very self-conscious when they are expected to talk to a pony but, like many other things, it is really just a habit, though an important one if you wish to become a good horseman or woman.

A sensible rider always checks his tack before he mounts. He takes a quick look to see that the saddle and bridle fit and have been put on properly, then he tightens his girths, pulls down his stirrups and mounts.

As you are too inexperienced to do this you will have to trust the person who saddled and bridled the pony for you and who will now tighten the girths, pull down the stirrups and hold the pony while you mount.

*How to mount*

The two important things to remember about mounting are not to stick your toe into the pony's stomach and not to land in the saddle with a bang and hurt his back. Naturally, if ponies are hurt each time they are mounted, they will soon begin to object, generally by biting or cow-kicking - that is kicking forward with a hind leg - so always be very careful.

Stand on the pony's left or near side. (If you are in any doubt about this it's the side on which the throat lash buckles.) Stand with your left shoulder close to his, you will be able to see his tail but not his head. Take the reins in your left hand and hold them just in front of the saddle. Take the stirrup in your right hand and put your left foot in it. The right hand now takes hold of the pummel - the front arch of the saddle - and you turn to face the saddle, pushing your toe down under the girth so that it doesn't dig into the pony. Then you spring up, pause for a moment in a standing position with your two legs together and your body leaning slightly over the saddle, before swinging the right leg over and sitting down gently in the saddle. You then put your right foot in the stirrup and the reins into two hands.

If you find the springing-up part of mounting very difficult, think about getting your head well over the pony's back towards the off-side as this will help you to put your weight in the right place. If your pony is too tall for you to mount you can let down the stirrup, mount from a mounting-block, box, upturned bucket or a gate or ask someone to give you a leg up, but a pony of a reasonable size is really essential when you are learning to mount.

*How to dismount*

To dismount, take both feet out of the stirrups, put the reins in the left hand and put it on the withers - the bony bit of pony just in front of the saddle. Take the pummel in the right hand and lean forward a little, then swing the right leg over the back or cantle of the saddle and jump down to the ground. Always take both feet out of the stirrups before you begin to dismount and beware of a rather superior-looking method in which the right leg is swung over the front of the saddle. This method can be dangerous on young or nervous ponies and also if you absent-mindedly attempt it while wearing a riding mac.

When mounting and dismounting the reins should be held just short enough to prevent the pony moving off. Never begin to mount with the reins in loops and the pony eating grass as he may set off at a gallop with you half on, or put a foot through the reins and break them.

*Does how you sit matter?*

The answer to this is yes, very much both to you and the pony. A rider who sits badly resembles a heavy school bag, especially at the faster paces when he bangs up and down on the pony's back, while a rider who sits well is more akin to a properly packed rucksack, fixed firmly to the shoulders. A rider with a good seat is able to keep his or her weight in the correct place all the time, no matter what the pony is doing, but the 'school bag' type of rider's weight is unpredictable - it turns up in unexpected places sometimes too far forward, but generally too far back, this unbalances the pony and upsets him.

Sitting in the correct position also allows the rider to have good hands. If you can sit still you can keep your hands still and only use them when you wish; you won't confuse your pony with involuntary signals.

A good seat goes with a correct leg position and this also enables the rider to give the leg aids or signals quickly and quietly; this is one of the secrets of having a willing and well-behaved pony.

If you have a good seat the exciting parts of riding, galloping, jumping and more advanced dressage will come easily to you, but, if you get into the habit of sitting badly, your riding career will be one long struggle as you try to do things in spite of your faults.

Begin by sitting in the lowest part of the saddle. If it is the right size for you there will be about a handsbreadth of saddle behind you. A great many people have bad seats because they sit too far back. When you are sitting in the correct place you can adjust your stirrups.

*The length of stirrups*

There are different lengths of stirrups for different forms of riding; long ones for dressage, short ones for jumping; very short ones for racing. To get the right length for ordinary riding hang your legs down when you are sitting in the lowest part of the saddle. The tread of the stirrup - the part on which your foot rests - should come about an inch below the knob of your ankle joint. If you are sitting either too far back, or on your fork rather than your seat bones, the measurement doesn't work.

When the stirrups are the correct length, put your feet in so that the ball of the foot is against the side of the iron further from the pony.

*Your leg position*

If you want to ride well you must have your legs under control; a common fault is having the legs too far forward. The inside of your knees should be against the saddle, but don't try to grip with them, and the lower leg, that is the part below the knee, should be drawn back so that the stirrup-leather hangs straight and is perpendicular to the ground.

Whatever length of stirrup you ride with, long or short, the correct position of the stirrup-leather is the same, for directly it leaves the perpendicular everything goes wrong. If the stirrup moves forward, your weight and seat are pushed backwards; and if the stirrup moves back, your weight is thrust forwards. It is a good idea to experiment with these three positions of the stirrup-leather so that you get the feel of the right one.

From the saddle you can check whether your legs are too far forward. Sit upright and take a quick look down, if your foot is in front of your knee your stirrup-leather can't be in the correct place. If you are inclined to ride with your legs too far forward, practise keeping your toes just out of sight; if you are inclined to ride with them too far back, practise keeping the tips of the toes just visible.

If it needs a great deal of effort to keep your legs back you are almost certainly sitting too far back in the saddle, so correct both faults at once; pushing your seat forward at the same time as you push your legs back.

Your heels should be lower than your toes, but don't try to force them down too hard as this will make you stiff, and your feet should be more or less straight with or parallel to the pony, but as people have differently shaped legs they cannot all manage exactly the same position; you will find that if your toes turn out too far your knees will come away from the saddle and this will be a bad fault when you begin to jump.

### *The rest of you*

When you are riding, always try to sit up and look proud. Try to be tall above the saddle and tall below, but don't try so hard that you become stiff.

Look up and about you and not down at your hands or at the ground. If you are trying to do something specific, like riding a circle or jumping a course, always look exactly where you want to go as the pony will feel the slight adjustment in your weight and be influenced by it rather in the same way as a bicycle is, but consciously.

*How to hold the reins*

Coming from the bit, the reins should enter your hand at the little finger end, cross the palm and emerge by the thumb which is bent at the knuckle and rests lightly on the rein. The hands are held about four inches apart with the thumbs uppermost and the finger-nails facing each other; they should be shut, but not tightly clenched and for ordinary riding the correct place for them is generally just above the pony's withers.

The real test of whether a rider's hands are in the right place for the particular horse he is riding, and for whatever he happens to be doing at a given moment, is whether there is a straight line from the bit along the rein through the rider's hands and forearm to his elbow.

This is a very important line and though the position of your hands and the pony's head will change according to what you are doing the line should still be straight. But don't get muddled and think that it must be a horizontal line, that would be quite wrong. It simply has to be straight without any kinks or breaks in it caused by you putting your hands too high or too low or by bending them in or out at the wrists. If there is not a straight line from the bit to your elbow, your hands will not be able to follow the pony's mouth and they will be hard and insensitive.

Don't hold the reins very short or grip them tightly. If you do, you will probably upset the pony. Later on, when you are secure in the saddle, you will learn to ride with contact with the pony's mouth but you can't do this yet. You must begin by riding with the reins just long enough to prevent you feeling the pony's mouth, but not so long that they hang in loops.

*Shortening the reins*

To shorten the reins, each hand has to help the other. The left hand, still holding it own rein, takes the spare end of the right rein above the right hand, which then slides forward down the rein. As soon as the right rein is short enough the right hand takes the left rein above the left hand and that hand slides forward. Always be careful to shorten the reins smoothly and gently otherwise you will hurt the pony's mouth.

For your first lesson you will either be on the leading rein or you will ride a very quiet pony in an enclosed space and he will follow his companions, so you won't really need the reins for stopping or steering purposes. Concentrate on sitting correctly and be careful to use the neckstrap, the pony's mane or the pummel of the saddle and not the reins for any holding on you may need to do.

*Moving off*

The signal, or in riding language the aid, to move forward is a gentle pressure against the pony's sides. It should be given by the inside of your lower leg, don't use the backs of your calves as this will make your toes turn out and your knees come away from the saddle. Begin with a gentle pressure of both legs and gradually increase it until he obeys, then relax your legs, this will tell him that he has done what you wanted. If he doesn't obey, try saying 'Walk on' and making a clicking noise with your tongue - this is better than becoming desperate and starting to kick. Remember that a pony will not move forward if you are holding him on a tight rein.

*To halt*

As a beginner riding with long reins you will have to shorten them before you ask the pony to halt, otherwise you will find that your hands are against your stomach before you have established contact with the pony's mouth.

The essential point to remember about halting is that you must use your legs. Riders who stop their mounts with the reins alone spoil the mouths of all the ponies they ride.

To stop, close the legs, that is press gently with the inside of both your legs as you did to move off, but at the same time feel the pony's mouth by increasing the tension on the reins. Sit up very straight and halt your own body instead of letting it follow the pony's stride. Don't pull on the reins and don't expect the pony to stop dead; all halts in riding should be made smoothly and slowly. Sudden rough halts from the faster paces not only hurt the pony's mouth they also cause tremendous strain to his legs and sometimes result in lameness.

If the pony doesn't seem to understand your aids, try saying Whoa or Halt in a long drawn-out voice.

If a pony makes a bad halt, that is if he throws his head up or opens his mouth wide or just stops with his hind legs straggling out behind him, it is generally because the rider has used too much hand and too little leg. You will find it very difficult at first to use exactly the right amount of each, but if you practise halting from the walk and watching how the pony reacts to your aids you will gradually learn. Remember that it is always better to use too much leg and too little rein than the other way round. A pony that has had his mouth spoiled by bad riding is very difficult to halt correctly, but if you go on giving the right aids he will eventually begin to improve, whereas if you resort to pulling he will only grow worse.

*Turning*

When you want to turn to the right you feel the right rein and use both legs, the left one a little farther back than its usual position. Once again, it will probably be necessary for the beginner to shorten his reins before he can feel the pony's mouth. As you feel the right rein the left hand must give a little so that the pony can turn his head and look the way he is going. But each hand must always remain on its own side of the neck; they must never cross over.

To turn to the left, you feel the left rein, give with the right hand and use both legs, pressing a little farther back than usual with the right one.

If you find it difficult to remember the aids when you are riding the pony, practise at home, using a chair as a mount and string for reins, until you get them all absolutely clear in your head.

*Trotting*

The aids to trot are the same as those to move off, a pressure of the inside of the calves of both legs.

A pony carries his head higher at the trot than he does at the walk and his neck becomes shorter so it will be necessary for you to shorten the reins a little before starting off.

You can rise to the trot or you can sit to it. Rising is the less tiring way for both pony and rider and is used out hacking and on journeys. Sitting is useful because it gives you a more complete control of the pony, but at first you will find sitting very uncomfortable, so, if you want to enjoy yourself, it is better to learn to rise as quickly as possible.

Rising isn't really very difficult provided that your legs remain in the right position; you merely lean slightly forward and try to stand in the stirrups and sit in the saddle alternately and in time with the pony's stride. At first it will seem hard work, but gradually you will find that the pony's action throws you up and that you don't need to do anything.

If it goes on being difficult and you feel that you are being left behind the pony and need to pull yourself up by the pummel or to push your stomach forward in order to rise then, almost certainly, your legs have come too far forward and your stirrup leathers are no longer perpendicular to the ground.

It is no use trotting on and on when you have lost your position in the saddle, bring the pony back to a walk, reorganize yourself with your legs in the right place and then try again.

### *Cantering*

A pony can canter with either his right foreleg or his left foreleg leading. When you give the aids to canter you tell him at the same time which leg he is to lead with. On a straight line it doesn't matter which leg he leads with, but if you are going to turn a corner or ride round in a circle he should lead with the inside leg.

To canter with the right or off foreleg leading, feel the right rein and press with both legs. When you are trotting it is important that you should stop rising and sit down in the saddle before you give the aids to canter, otherwise the pony will probably just trot faster and faster. If you are worried about getting him on the correct leg ask him to canter as you come into a corner as most ponies will then strike off on the correct leg of their own accord.

The aids to canter with the near or left foreleg leading are sit down in the saddle, feel the left rein and press with both legs.

If a pony is not very well-trained and it is difficult to start him on a particular leg then you can use your outside leg farther back than usual as though you were turning a corner. Going round to the right you would canter with the off fore leading, therefore you would feel the right rein and it would be your left leg that was used farther back than usual.

*The seat at the canter*

There are two ways of sitting at the canter, one way is used for hacking, showing and dressage, and the other for jumping and cross-country riding. In this country most people learn the ordinary, more sedate seat first and the forward seat when they begin to jump. At the ordinary canter you should sit upright and look just as comfortable and relaxed as you do when riding at the walk. But this isn't easy, especially if you have a pony with a rough canter. Try to sit deep into your pony, be careful to keep your legs in the correct position and do your best to prevent your back going stiff as this is what causes you to bounce up and down. If you feel like holding on, use the pummel of the saddle, the mane or the neckstrap - but on no account the reins.

*Riding without stirrups*

Riding without stirrups is the best way to learn to canter. Try first of all at the walk. Simply cross your stirrups over the pony's withers, in front of the saddle. Put a knot about one-third of the way up your reins - by making a loop in the reins and passing the buckle end through it - if the knot is in the right place it will lie on the pony's neck just in front of the withers. If you take the reins at or near the knot you will find that you can control the pony easily with one hand, which leaves the other hand free to help you keep a correct seat by holding the pummel of the saddle.

Keeping the correct seat is extremely important, riding badly without stirrups, bumping miserably up and down in the wrong part of the saddle will not improve you at all. Sit as usual in the centre of the saddle and let your knees and heels go as low as they will without losing your upright position.

If you begin to tip forward, it is a sign that you are trying to ride with too long a leg and have begun to sit on your fork instead of your seat-bones. A fork seat is a weak and useless seat, so be careful to avoid this. When you feel at home at the walk, without stirrups, try a gentle trot. Hold on to the pummel, keep your legs in the correct place and don't try to stay in the saddle by gripping with your calves.

Once you can trot without stirrups, cantering without them is easy, so you will no longer be worried by losing a stirrup while cantering, but the awkward moment and the one when most beginners fall off, is the transition or change from the canter to the trot. Some ponies make this transition very badly. They change from quite a fast canter into a fast, rough and unbalanced trot and their riders roll off like leaves in autumn.

If you have a pony like this you will have to do a lot of stirrup-less riding because the only real cure is for the rider to develop a deep and secure seat, he can then help the pony to remain balanced by keeping his hind-legs under him and enabling him to change from a slow canter to a slow trot. Until you have a firm enough seat to do this you will just have to slow up his canter as much as you can and then, as he breaks into a trot, put the reins in one hand and grab the neck strap or the pummel.

When in difficulties about slowing up or stopping, always remember to use your voice, but don't forget that Whoa, Go and No sound very alike to ponies, it is only in the way that they are said that they become different.

*Likely difficulties*

Ponies that are ridden by beginners generally have three faults. They eat grass at all sorts of inconvenient moments, they are rather lazy and slow to answer your leg aids and they are nappy, that is they take you back to the field gate or to other ponies or even to their stables, when you don't want to go there at all.

*Grazing*

This is quite easily cured. A cord tied to the ring of the snaffle, passed through the little loop which joins the browband to the headpiece of the bridle and then tied to a D on the front of the saddle, can be made just tight enough to prevent the pony reaching the grass.

While a cord is the answer for very young riders, older and larger beginners will find that if they shorten their reins and use their legs the pony can be prevented from getting his head down and once he learns that he is not going to be allowed to eat he will give up trying. Always remember to untie anti-grazing cords before jumping as otherwise the pony may not have the full freedom of his head and neck.

*Obeying the legs*

Persuading a beginner's pony to answer a reasonably light leg aid is a more difficult problem, since ponies which are sensitive to the aids are quite unsuitable for early riding lessons as they become upset by the unintentional and meaningless signals which the beginner gives each time he loses his balance. But this does not mean that beginners' ponies have to be kicked along by the riders' heels. In fact, the more they are kicked the more sluggish they will become, for kicking has a deadening effect on ponies.

The answer is to carry a whip, as soon as you can manage it. Don't hit the pony with it, but use it to draw his attention to your leg aids. When you squeeze with both legs, telling him to move off or break into a trot, and nothing happens, put the reins quietly in one hand, take the whip in the other and give him a tap just behind your leg on that side.

Experienced riders use a very long whip when training a young horse as they can then give him a tap without the need to put the reins in one hand; but it takes several years to learn to ride well enough to manage a long whip properly and, meanwhile, you should make absolutely certain that you always put your reins in one hand before you use the whip in the other. Using a whip in the same hand as the rein generally means a jerk in the mouth for the pony, so as well as hurting him, you are asking him to go faster and slower at the same time. This naturally muddles him and makes him sullen and sluggish.

The idea we want to get into the pony's head is that if he obeys the rider's legs he won't get a tap with the whip. In other words use a light aid first and then increase its severity until he obeys. It's really common sense: don't begin by being rude and kicking, ask politely first, using the proper leg aids, and see if you are obeyed.

If you are the only person who rides the pony the improvement will probably be quite startling, but if he is a riding school pony and the other pupils are allowed to kick you can't hope for any permanent result; you will, however, have a very much less exhausting ride if you refuse to kick and you will avoid the risk of getting into a bad habit.

*Napping*

Nappy ponies are generally just trying to see how much disobedience they can get away with. As soon as they find that their rider can stop them dashing off to the gate or to the other ponies they stop napping. If you are not a very good rider it needs brains to outwit them. First of all, get in the habit of leaving the napping area briskly and coming back to it slowly. Many beginners encourage nappiness by doing just the opposite. Make sure that you trot away from the gate and trot back. And, never, even if it's pouring with rain or you're twenty minutes late, never go galloping back to the stable at the end of a lesson. A good rider always walks his horse in.

The famous Greek rider Xenophon, writing three hundred years before the birth of Christ, knew all about nappiness and he advised his readers to dismount on the schooling ground and lead their horses in. But, whether you lead them or ride them, it is the sign of a thoroughly bad rider to take a pony back to his stable at a faster pace than a walk.

Some ponies begin to go sideways like crabs as soon as they enter the napping area and when this happens the rider must sit down and use his or her legs and seat; the leg on the side which the pony is napping to should be used a little farther back than usual. The way you use your reins on a napping pony is very important. Suppose he is napping to the left and you have asked him to go to the right, you have given your aids - right rein, both legs, left one back a little - and you must go on giving the same aids no matter what the pony does. If you change over and circle him round to the left because that seems easier the pony will think that he has won the battle even if he didn't reach his friends or the gate. And, as long as he thinks he can win, he will go on having napping fits at inconvenient moments. So, when you give an aid, stick to it until it's obeyed; even if you can only ride round and round in tiny circles on the right rein you will be doing far more good than if you change over and use the left.

# CHAPTER THREE

## RIDING IN A SCHOOL

Riding on the straight up and down a field or going out for hacks in the countryside are good ways of learning to sit correctly at the walk, trot and canter. Hacking will help you to relax and get the feel of your pony, and, in a country district where you can leave the roads and go for miles through fields and woods, it will give you a great deal of pleasure. But if you want to improve and become a good rider, hacking is not enough; you have to ride in the school.

In riding language, a school is just a flat space where horses and riders are trained. It can be a covered school, a huge building with a soft tan floor, or an outdoor school which is fenced, usually drained in some way to prevent it becoming boggy in winter and generally has an all weather surface. Or it can be just a corner of a field with a few markers - letters, oil-drums, big stones or posts - to show the riders where to go. Schools are oblong and if you mark one out for yourself it should not be less than twenty metres by forty metres.

*Keeping your distance*

Out hacking it is quite easy to drift along with your pony following the others, but in a school, especially when riding in a ride, that is a class with other riders, you have to be alert all the time. First of all you must keep your pony one pony's length behind the pony in front of you. This is called keeping your distance and if you don't keep it you may be kicked or your pony may tread on the other pony's heels and lame him.

Don't try to keep your distance by constantly changing your speed or pace. Do your best to ride at exactly the same speed as the pony in front but, if this is impossible, make use of the corners going as wide as possible if you want to slow down and cutting them a little if you want to catch up.

*Riding round corners*

It is important to ride each corner properly, giving the aids for turning and making sure that the pony goes round it correctly, bending his body, and looking in the direction in which he is going. Some ponies can't bend their bodies because they haven't been properly schooled and it is much easier for them to cut the corners than to go round correctly. If you have a stiff pony you must try to improve him gradually, asking him to go a little more into the corners each day but on no account should you try to force him into them by using the outside rein.

Imagine that you are going round the school to the left. The pony should look inwards at every corner when you use your legs and feel the left rein. If he is cutting the corners and you try to prevent him by using your right or outside rein he will turn his head outwards. If he does this he will go stiffer than ever and his cornering will become worse instead of better. To prevent him cutting corners you can only use the inside leg.

Besides being uncomfortable to ride, stiff ponies are not as safe as supple ponies; they are much more likely to fall when going round corners on a wet and slippery day. There are other disadvantages too, they can't cut corners in show-jumping competitions and so lose valuable seconds when jumping off against the clock, and they collect very few marks in dressage competitions as the judges consider it a very serious fault.

### *More about the walk*

The walk is a pace of four-time. The pony moves each of his legs separately and if he is walking on the road you can hear four distinct hoof-beats. A good walk is a quiet, even, long-striding one and the pony will move with a long neck and need a fairly long rein. Bad walkers dawdle, take short quick steps or jog. Jogging is often caused by the rider having his reins too short or too tight.

*Overtracking*

When a pony is walking well his hind hoof prints will come in front of those left by his fore hoofs. An indifferent walker will place his hind hoofs on the prints of the fore hoofs, while a bad walker's hind hoofs will not even reach them. It is very easy to tell whether other people's ponies are walking well and you can judge your own by looking down at the hoof prints when riding on soft ground.

To get your pony walking well press with each of your calves in turn, in time with his stride. If he is lazy a tap with the whip may persuade him to attend to you and is far better than kicking.

*More about the trot*

The trot is a pace of two-time. The pony moves his legs in diagonal pairs near-fore and off-hind together and the off-fore with the near-hind. On the road you will hear the four hoofs land with only two hoof-beats because they come down in pairs. The diagonals are known by their forelegs, so the near-fore and off-hind are called the left or near diagonal and the off-fore and near-hind are the off or right diagonal.

When you are expert at rising to the trot it is a good plan to change your diagonal fairly often so that you don't always either rise or sit to the same pair of legs. To change, you simply sit down for two beats instead of one and then rise again. Old ponies which have been used to riders who rose always to the same diagonal may feel rather rough and uncomfortable and some will even try to change you back again by giving a shy or stumbling. However, it is worth going against their wishes as later on, for more advanced riding, it is an advantage to be equally at home on either diagonal and you won't be unless you get into the habit of riding on them both now.

A good trot is slow and steady with a regular rhythm but long-striding and energetic. Short quick, scurrying steps are a sign of bad balance on the part of the pony; he has too much weight on his forehand. A fast trot is a sign of a bad rider, especially on the roads as the jar of slapping his feet down on the hard surface may give the pony one of the incurable lamenesses.

*The sitting trot*

Experienced riders do a great deal of their schooling at the sitting trot as it enables them to bring their horses' hind legs farther under their bodies which is essential for collected work. You will begin by finding it useful for striking off into a canter, for circling and for giving you more control if your pony plays up or shies, but you will not reap any advantages from it until you can sit without effort; bumping up and down is equally uncomfortable for you and the pony.

To sit to the trot without effort, a correct seat is essential. Whether you practise with or without stirrups, you must sit deeply into your saddle with your legs in the right place, and your body upright. You must not grip with your knees or calves for, though this would stop you bouncing up and down it will make you sit on top of your saddle instead of into it and as, in this position you have no influence over your pony's hind legs, the whole object of riding at the sitting trot will be lost.

Begin by practising for short distances and, when you lose the correct seat, help yourself back into it by holding the pummel of the saddle.

If your pony is very young, thin or unfit always use the rising trot until he is stronger and has developed his back muscles with work.

*More about the canter*

The canter is a slow gallop. It became known as the canter in English because it was the pace at which the pilgrims rode across the downs to Canterbury; at first it was called the Canterbury gallop and then this was shortened to canter.

The canter is a pace of three-time and either foreleg can lead. If the near foreleg leads, the off-hind is the first hoof to the ground then the off-fore and the near-hind together and lastly the leading leg. The pony is then in the air for a moment before he begins the next stride with the off-hind.

There are two ways of changing the leading leg. One is to bring the pony back to a walk or trot and then re-start him on the other leg, this is called the simple or ordinary change of leg, the other method - the flying change - is done at the moment of the canter when the pony is in the air. To do this correctly and to order needs an experienced rider on a highly trained horse, but most ponies change legs naturally whenever they change direction. If your pony doesn't or if he only changes in front and not behind, which is called cantering disunited, bring him back to a trot and restart him on the correct leg. You will realize that the pony is disunited because the canter will suddenly become very rough and uncomfortable; always slow up to a trot at once as if you let him go on it can become a habit.

*Which leg is he on?*

If you watch someone else's pony cantering you will see that the two forelegs seem to come forward at the same moment but that one always comes farther forward than the other, this is the leading leg. It is more difficult to tell which leg you're on when you are mounted, especially as you are not supposed to lean forward and look down. At first you will have to look down at the pony's knees, but try to make it a quick look, don't canter for miles in this position and don't start looking down until the pony is cantering or you will upset his balance as he strikes off. As soon as you can tell which leg he is on by the knees try to tell from his shoulders as this will cause much less movement on your part. Later on, when you are more expert, you will find that you can tell the leading leg by feel and without looking at all.

*The counter-lead*

Though cantering round corners on the wrong leg can cause a half-schooled pony to fall, especially if the ground is slippery, well-schooled horses are taught to canter on the wrong leg when asked and this is called the counter-lead. In fairly advanced dressage tests serpentines and circles have to be made at the counter-canter, but it is not a good exercise for inexperienced riders or for any but the most highly-trained ponies.

*Cantering disunited*

When a pony canters disunited his forelegs and hindlegs follow each other in the wrong order.

Imagine that you set off at the canter with the near-fore leading, then you turn to the right and the pony changes his forelegs, but, not being very well balanced, he fails to change behind. He is now cantering with his forelegs moving in the order for a right canter while his hind legs follow the order for a left canter. From the saddle this feels very odd and rough almost as though the pony had suddenly gone lame. If you watch someone else's pony cantering united, that is correctly, you will see that the leading foreleg and the hind leg on the same side look as though they come forward together. If a pony is cantering disunited it is the hind leg on the opposite side that appears to come forward with the leading leg.

In the school you should never go round a corner on the wrong leg and hope the pony will change, always bring him back to a trot and restart him on the correct leg. When showjumping or when riding in gymkhana events, there isn't time for this and you have to hope that your pony will change legs of his own accord. He is much more likely to do this if you make a habit of seeing that he always canters on the correct leg in the school and out hacking.

*The dangers of cantering slowly*

A good canter is slow and long-striding. The pony should look elegant and full of life and yet be light in hand, he mustn't pull or lean heavily on the bit. But a pony can only canter like this if he has had a lot of schooling and developed the muscles of his hind-quarters. If you try to make a pony canter very slowly before he has developed the right muscles, you will find that you have to hold him back with the reins, and holding ponies back with the reins is akin to driving a car or riding a bicycle with the brakes on, and not at all good for him. Ponies which have been made to canter slowly before they were ready to do so have lifeless, pottering canters and instead of their hind legs coming well under their bodies they trail along behind.

If your pony canters too fast is it perfectly all right to use your reins and legs together to slow him up and show him the pace at which you would like to canter, but as soon as he obeys and slows up you must relax your hands; you mustn't ride along with the brakes on.

Very well-schooled horses and ponies can canter at walking pace, but most ordinary ponies have natural canters that are rather faster than a brisk trot; to teach them to canter slower you practise riding large circles about the size of half your school.

Young horses are not well enough balanced to canter while carrying a rider until they have been schooled at the walk and trot for some time, generally about three months from the time they were broken in. They can be given a quiet gallop out hacking without coming to any harm, but forcing them to canter round a school before they are ready can spoil their mouths and their natural canters as they will not be able to use their hind legs properly.

*The gallop*

To gallop you merely press your pony on out of a canter. You should remain in control and keep him between the hands and legs and balanced. Don't encourage him to go flat out, that is as fast as he can - and don't race him. Ponies can so easily become silly and hysterical over galloping and you don't want to find that you've turned into one of those riders who daren't go out of a collected canter in case their pony runs away. If you ride sensibly there is no need for the gallop to be any less controlled than the other paces and it mustn't be if you want to ride across country, jumping at speed and going down steep hills without slowing up.

But don't think that riding the pony between hand and leg means that you have to hold him back on a tight rein, on the contrary, you want him to go quietly and easily - 'well within himself', which means with a reserve of speed and energy so that you could ask him to go faster if you wanted to - but not pulling or fighting for his head which would only make both of you tired. If the pony gallops too fast, slow him up to the speed you want, using your hands and legs together and relaxing the aids the moment he obeys exactly as you would at the trot or canter. You may have to slow him up again a few moments later, but it doesn't matter how often you have to use your hands and legs provided you reward him by relaxing the aids each time he obeys.

*The seat at the gallop*

As the pony goes faster his body becomes long and lower and he stretches his neck out. To keep in balance with him you lean forward and shorten your reins. If you pull up your stirrups two or three holes before galloping and ride with the jumping or cross-country seat you will find the sensation of speed much greater and more enjoyable.

Until you get used to galloping, always allow yourself plenty of time and space in which to stop and try to arrange to have your first gallop either uphill or along a stretch of grass with a hill at the end. Don't gallop fat or unfit ponies, don't gallop on hard ground and don't gallop through deep - very muddy - going if this can be avoided as your pony may sprain a tendon especially if he is already tired.

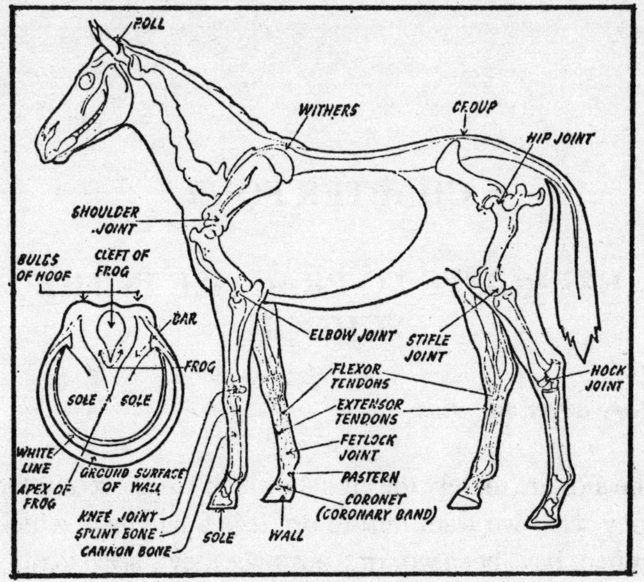


Some points of the horse.

# CHAPTER FOUR

# EXERCISES TO PRACTISE IN THE SCHOOL

*More about the aids*

The aids are merely the signals which we use to tell the pony what we want him to do. It is a language which humans have been working out since they started to ride. Xenophon wrote about the aids and one can still read books, published in England four hundred years ago, which explain how a horse should be taught them, only in those days they were called helpes. Probably, in less civilized times, the information was passed from generation to generation by word of mouth.

It would be quite possible to ignore these aids and to teach a pony to answer a completely different set of signals known only to his owner. But this would hardly be fair on the pony who would have a miserable time if he was ever sold and ridden by other people. It would be as though your parents had taught you a private language instead of English and then sent you to work or to school.

Another reason for using the accepted aids is that generations of good horsemen have thought about them and tried to produce signals which can be given without a lot of movement on the part of the rider and which are easy for the horse to understand and obey. Once a horse or pony has learned to move away from the legs and to slow up when the reins are felt the aids for the various movements become sensible and logical; our aids show him what we want; they position him each time we use them; he doesn't have to remember a lot of unrelated signals.

Apart from learning the aids for any movement you wish to carry out you must learn how to give them. The secret of having an obedient pony is to give always the lightest possible aid, then increase its severity until the pony obeys and the moment he does you cease to give it so that he knows he has done what you wanted.

Unfortunately, it is impossible to give the aids as perfectly as this without a good position, a firm seat and your hands and legs in the correct places. If your legs are too far forward you will always give your leg aids too late and too hard. If you are in the habit of riding with your toes turned out and the backs of your calves against the pony you won't be able to stop giving the leg aids when he obeys them. If you ride with your hands below the level of the rein, that is you break the straight line from the bit to the rider's elbow by carrying your hands too low, you will be riding with the brakes slightly on all the time and so the pony will no longer answer a light rein aid.

A pony that is given rough aids either becomes hopelessly excitable or he grows insensitive and answers only rough aids. If you teach your pony to answer light aids you will find him a more enjoyable ride and also you will be able to keep your more severe aids in reserve for emergencies. If it needs all your strength and energy to stir your pony into a trot you will have nothing in reserve when you have to persuade him to trot past some terrifying object.

When riding strange ponies it is very important to give the lightest possible aids and to ride with rather a long rein until you find out what sort of pony you are on. Well-bred ponies are generally thin-skinned and sensitive and if they are given rough aids or held on a tight rein they can become upset to the point where they don't know what they are doing and go almost berserk.

Remember that kicking, pulling, tugging and jerking are not aids but exhibitions of bad riding and that while bad riders manage to make riding look hair-raising and difficult as they battle with disobedient ponies, good riders make it look smooth and easy and their ponies always seem happy to oblige.

*Changing the rein*

It is dull for a pony, and for a rider, to go round and round the school in the same direction or, as it is called in riding language, on the same rein. A good horseman changes the rein every few minutes.

Obviously there are lots of ways of turning the pony round, but as the whole object of schooling is to improve the pony and rider you never turn suddenly or sharply as you might in an emergency, but always gradually and smoothly taking care that the pony doesn't lose his rhythm and balance , throw up his head, or shorten his stride. The most usual way to change direction in a school, especially if you are being taught in a ride with other people, is by riding diagonally across the school from quarter-marker to quarter-marker, but this can only be done from the first quarter-marker you come to after riding round one of the short sides. Always begin changes of direction in plenty of time, ride the pony round using the legs as well as the reins and then make sure that he has the correct bend, that is he is looking to the inside, for the first corner on the new rein.

*Circles*

Large circles are a very good exercise to practise as they make ponies supple and supple ponies are far more pleasant to ride and far easier to control than stiff ones. Well-schooled ponies can make quite small circles, but a stiff or badly balanced pony can't, however hard he tries. If you force him to attempt them you will only make him stiffer than ever and he may become sour: one of those ponies that hates being schooled because it has all been made too difficult for him and goes along with his ears back, his tail swishing and a miserable expression on his face.

Half your school is a good size for a circle and practise at a walk until you get the idea of it and then at the trot which is better for the pony.

To circle correctly a pony must bend his body behind his shoulder; this will allow his hind legs to follow exactly the same path as his forelegs and his whole body to follow the curve of the circle. If you draw a circle and then add a picture of a straight pony going round it you will see at once that a straight pony can't make a circle but only a square. He must be curved; the larger the circle the slighter the curve, which is why you begin with large ones.

*The aids for circling*

Always mark your circle out in your mind's eye before you begin to ride it. Choose the centre and then watch it out of the corner of your eye, this will help you to keep the same distance away all the time and will prevent the circle from becoming banana-shaped. As the circle is a slight but continuous turn you have to give the aids to turn all the time you are circling: that is you feel the inside rein, give enough with the outside hand to allow the pony to bend his neck slightly inwards while keeping contact, use the outside leg behind the girth and the inside leg in the usual place. But as you grow more experienced and ride well-schooled ponies you will find that these rather obvious aids become unnecessary, the movement of the rider's body as he looks towards the centre of his circle together with the lightest of rein aids will put a supple pony on the circle, while the rider's legs and seat keep him going at exactly the correct pace with aids that are invisible to the bystanders.

Though the rider turns his shoulders to look inwards he must always remain upright and never lean inwards or outwards. If the pony begins to lean inwards and take short, quick steps the circle is too small for his stage of schooling and he should practise larger ones until he is better balanced and more supple.

Beware of using too much inside rein and having a pony with a very bent neck and a straight body, what you want is a pony that is very slightly curved from nose to tail.

Beware also of trying to prevent a pony cutting in and making the circle too small with the outside rein. If you do this he will look to the outside, circling will become impossible, and he will grow more stiff instead of less. To make a circle bigger or to prevent a pony cutting-in use the inside aids, particularly the inside leg.

*Halting from the trot and canter*

Many riders make the mistake of thinking that the reins are brakes and that if they pull hard enough their ponies are bound to stop, this is not so. Imagine someone sitting on your back pulling at a bit in your mouth. He could certainly hurt you by jerking or pulling on the reins, but he wouldn't be able to make you stop against your will. If he made a habit of hurting your mouth it would either become hard and insensitive in which case you could ignore all his rein aids, or you would be so frightened of having it hurt that you would try to carry your head so that your mouth was out of contact with the rider's hands. This is what star-gazers, those ponies which carry their heads thrown back and their faces looking up at the sky, are doing.

Ponies which are ridden on tight rein are inclined to pull with their heads down. This is only an attempt to relieve their aching neck muscles, but, like star-gazing, it quickly becomes a habit.

The important thing to remember about stopping is that the rein aid is only a signal to stop which a well-schooled pony obeys if he is not too wildly excited and provided he is in a position to obey. A pony can't stop quickly and easily if he is unbalanced.

Everyone knows the feeling of running downhill and the moment when you begin to run faster and faster and you simply can't stop because your weight has gone too far forward and you're unbalanced. Ponies mostly have quite good natural balance, but this is upset when they have to carry a rider and one of the main reasons for schooling your horses and ponies is to develop the muscles that will make them able to remain balanced while carrying a rider's weight. But afterwards, all through the pony's life, the rider has to help him to keep balanced.

No amount of pulling on the reins will stop an unbalanced pony that is going fast. The rider has to sit down in the saddle and use his legs and seat to push the pony's hind legs farther under him so that they take their share of the weight.

To learn to do this you and the pony must practise halting first from the walk then from the trot and then, when you can manage this smoothly and easily, from the canter and gallop. To halt from the walk, shorten the reins if you have been riding with a long or loose rein, feel the pony's mouth, close your legs - without turning your toes out - and by sitting up very straight let your weight go down into your heels and bring your back into use.

Give the pony plenty of time to stop. If you hurry him he will stop in the middle of a stride with his legs scattered about instead of at the end of a stride with his forelegs level and both his hind legs under his body. In riding language, he should halt 'square' and, when he does, relax your aids for this will show him that he has done what you wanted.

From the trot you use the same aids to halt, but in order to use your back, you have to stop rising and sit down. At first you will find that you need to walk for quite a long way before you actually halt, but gradually as you become more experienced and your pony becomes better trained you will find that the strides you need to take at the walk grow less and less. It takes an experienced horse and rider to halt directly from the trot, and if you try to do this too soon you will use too much hand and instead of coming to a smooth halt with a steady head-carriage your pony will have to throw his head up or down or open his mouth in an attempt to get relief from your severe aids. As he does this his back will go stiff and so his hind-legs won't be able to come under him.

In fact a severe rein aid makes everything go wrong and the pony gradually becomes more difficult to stop as he develops the wrong muscles of his neck and body.

If your pony has already been spoiled by someone else you will be able to improve him if you practise a lot of halting from the walk, using the lightest possible rein aids, but it takes time and it is important not to race him or otherwise excite him until you have him in the habit of halting correctly, for every time you are forced to use rough aids to stop him you undo at least a week of your schooling.

Don't think that martingales or severe bits or tight nosebands and curb-chains will make your pony easier to stop. By making him afraid of having his mouth hurt they may seem to improve things for a day or two, but they can't develop his muscles or improve his balance, only schooling can do that.

It takes a good rider on a well-schooled pony to halt directly from the canter. The dashing-looking halts that cowboys make in films are hard on a pony's mouth and on his legs and shouldn't be attempted if you value him.

At first you will have to break from a canter into a trot and then into a walk before halting, but as you become more expert you will find that it is comparatively easy to canter from a walk and to walk from a canter without any steps at the trot.

If halting from a walk seems to you rather a dull occupation to practise for months on end remember that you and the pony are both learning a great deal from it. He is learning to keep his head steady and to bring his hind legs under his body and developing the muscles which will enable him to halt quickly from the faster paces; you are learning to use your back, to feel his stride and to use your hands in a sensitive manner, three essentials for a good rider.

### *The turn on the forehand*

The turn on the forehand is an exercise which all riders and all ponies should learn to do. It is an easy but not very exciting movement which teaches the pony to move sideways away from the leg and gives the rider control of his quarters. A pony which can make a turn on the forehand is much handier than one which cannot. He is much better at opening gates, he's easier to keep straight in traffic and it is a simple matter to turn his heels away from dogs, people or other horses if you want to let them pass on a narrow track.

The turn on the forehand is only made from the halt, but it is a good plan to have been walking briskly just before you halted and to move off into a brisk walk the moment you've finished the turn. If you ask a pony to do any exercise when he has been standing for some time and is half asleep he is sure to do it badly.

It is usual to make half a turn on the forehand, which means that you finish facing in the opposite direction from which you began, but if your pony has never made one before you begin by asking him for one step, then you gradually work up to a quarter and finally to a half-turn.

During the turn the pony's forelegs must remain on the same spot. He can either mark time with them or pivot round on the inner leg. Imagine that you have drawn a small circle round his forelegs with a piece of chalk; at the end of the movement they must still be in that circle and they must not have left it, if they did you haven't made a turn on the forehand at all. Only the hind legs move sideways; they walk round in quiet even steps.

The aids for the right turn on the forehand, that is when the pony moves his quarters round to the left, are to feel both reins - this tells him not to walk forward - the right one a fraction stronger than the left. The well-schooled horse then flexes his jaw and turns his head very slightly to the right. Your right leg, pressing a little farther back than usual, tells him to move his quarters to the left while your left leg remains in its usual place ready to check him if he begins to move backwards, to tell him when he has taken as many steps as you want and to join the right leg in sending him forward at the end of the movement.

As usual, make your aids as light as you can. Relax your leg each time you feel that the pony is about to obey it and make a step and then press again for the next one.

Beginners generally make the mistake of using too much rein. When the pony fails to answer the leg aid they become frantic and pull his head round with the rein thus actually *telling* him to move his forehand, the very thing we are trying to avoid. So keep an eye on your hands, but don't look down, lean forward, twist your body or put your legs too far back, all of which will make it far harder for you to persuade the pony to do what you want. Sit up and give the aids correctly. If the pony fails to obey, a light tap with the whip just behind your leg should draw his attention to the aid. If this makes no impression, standing him beside a wall or fence and asking him to move his quarters away from it may help him to understand what you want. Otherwise a dismounted friend who will push with a hand just behind your leg, generally explains things.

If you have no dismounted friend and the pony won't move even one rather grudging step in the right direction don't sit on him giving frantic and incorrect aids, dismount, take both reins in one hand, as close to his chin as your length of arm will let you, and push his quarters away from you using the other hand where your leg would be if you were mounted. If he ignores the press of your hand of swings his quarters towards you you will have to tap him with the whip. Difficult ponies should practise this every time they are tied up to be groomed or saddled. Get him in the habit of moving his quarters away from you each time you say 'Get over' and press his flank with your hand.

Pushing a pony round doesn't produce a very good turn on the forehand, but it does give a stubborn or unwieldy pony the right idea and later on you can say 'Get over' when you ask for a proper turn mounted.

The aids for the left turn on the forehand are, of course, the opposite to the ones for the right. A slight extra feel on the left rein, the left leg a little farther back than usual while the right rein and leg keep contact ready to tell the pony that he should not go forwards or backwards.

Once you and the pony have mastered the turn on the forehand and can do it easily and quietly there is no need to go on practising it, for, once he has learned to move his quarters, the turn won't improve him any more; it won't improve his balance or develop his muscles in the same way as circling and halting.

*The rein-back*

Most riders and most ponies rein-back very badly.

There are several important points to look for if you watch anyone reining-back. First the pony should go back willingly and with impulsion - that is energy. But he must remain under the rider's control and not rush backwards. He should take quiet steady steps, keep straight and be ready to move forward again as soon as he is asked. Then watch his legs. The rein-back is a pace of two-time; the pony must go backwards by moving his diagonally opposite legs in pairs as though he was trotting and not in four-time, moving each leg separately, as in the walk. Finally, he must have a steady head-carriage; his head should remain in the correct position for a halt and not be thrown up or down; he should not overbend nor open his mouth wide.

*The aids for the rein-back*

To rein-back, close the legs a little farther back than usual and press the pony forward at the same time feel the reins just enough to prevent him going forward, and say 'Back' in a reasonably loud and drawn-out voice. If your pony doesn't understand, place him so that he faces a wall, fence or hedge and try again, but make sure that the obstacle is too high for him to jump. If he still doesn't understand don't become excited and begin to use rough leg aids, ask a friend to stand in front of him and tap him gently on the knees with your whip while you give the aids and you both say 'Back'. If you haven't a friend around at that moment, dismount and do the knee-tapping yourself. Pat and praise the pony each time he takes a step, however grudging and small, and remember to say 'Back' for each step so that when you mount again he will understand what you want him to do and gradually he will connect the proper aids with the word.

The fatal mistake in reining-back is to pull on the reins. Once you start trying to pull your pony backwards his head will go up, throwing extra weight on the hind-legs, and the movement will become very difficult for him. He may go backwards, but he'll only take small grudging steps in four-time, whereas he should back in two-time, moving his diagonal legs together in pairs, as he does at the trot.

After you've reined-back always ride your pony forward immediately as this will prevent him losing his impulsion or getting in the bad habit of running backwards. For the same reason always decide the number of steps you mean to back before you begin and don't let the pony take any more.

Ponies which have their weight on their forehands and carry their heads low will not be harmed and may be improved by quite a lot of reining-back, but it is not a good exercise for young ponies, very excitable ponies or those which carry their heads too high and they shouldn't practise too often. Ponies which run backwards when they are napping or over-excited shouldn't practise it at all.

When reining-back, the rider should always sit up straight and look ahead. He should have the feel that he is riding his pony forward into a hand that says 'No', rather than that he is making his pony go backwards.

# CHAPTER FIVE

# PROBLEM PONIES

Some ponies are much more difficult to ride and to school than others. Like people, ponies are different shapes and conformation makes a great deal of difference to the way in which a pony moves, carries his head and to whether he has good or bad natural balance. Intelligent schooling can improve and sometimes cure faults caused by poor conformation, it will also make all but the most hideous ponies better-looking. On the other hand, bad riding can ruin the best made ponies; it can give them every sort of fault and change their conformation so much that even a champion of the show-ring can be made to look nondescript.

The problems which follow are common ones and can be caused by poor conformation, bad riding or lack of schooling.

*An unbalanced canter*

Some ponies have such bad balance at the canter they are almost impossible to canter round a school. If the school is in the open they are always outside the markers and if it is enclosed they refuse to canter at all as they know that they are too unbalanced to get round the corners of such a confined space and they are afraid of falling.

These ponies generally have poor conformation; straight shoulders, a heavy badly set-on neck or a large head or sometimes quarters which are higher than their withers - all faults which throw too much weight on the forehand. The way to get the weight off the forehand is by schooling at the trot; by making plenty of turns, changes of direction and circles while riding at a smooth, steady, but energetic trot. A fast-scurrying trot or a smooth lifeless one won't do.

The next stage is to practise a lot of halting from the trot and trotting from the halt, but this will be no good unless the transitions - changes of pace - are made very smoothly, through the walk, and without kicking or pulling by the rider.

If the pony has been spoiled and carries his head low, reining-back will help to improve him; but if he is young he won't have enough muscle for this sort of work and he oughtn't to be asked to canter round the school, but only on the straight while out hacking until he is older and fitter.

Cantering on the long sides and trotting round the short sides of the school is also a good exercise for ponies that are inclined to become unbalanced.

*Ponies which won't stop*

If you can't stop your pony you may find yourself being advised to ride him in a more severe bit. If your pony is a young one - under six - ignore the advice as it is quite wrong to ride young ponies in any bits but smooth, thick snaffles; if, however, he is an older pony that has been spoiled it may be worth considering the matter.

Ponies which pull with their heads down can be ridden in double bridles quite successfully because there are two bits which have separate reins and this allows the rider to use the snaffle - or as it is often called, the bridoon - most of the time and the more severe and downward acting curb when it is needed, but bits such as pelhams, with only one mouthpiece and a curb chain, have a down wind action and encourage a lower head carriage.

The curb bit of a double bridle is a very severe bit and should not be used on its own, twisted and roughened bits are designed to hurt the pony's mouth and should not be used.

Remember that the more you hurt your pony the worse his mouth will become and the real cure for a pony which pulls with his head down is to improve your seat and then school him until his balance is better and his hindlegs will come farther under his body.

*Star-gazers*

Ponies which pull with their heads in the air are called star-gazers. Generally they have good natural balance, are courageous and sensitive, but their conformation, that is the way in which they are made, has given them a tendency to star-gazing. They have rather light necks and the top, or crest, is not muscular enough. Sometimes they have ewe necks which means that the top line of the crest is concave instead of convex. If, when he is young, this sort of pony is ridden carefully and quietly by a rider who never forgets to use his legs whenever he uses his reins the pony will gradually develop the muscles along the top of his neck and the tendency to star-gaze will disappear. But if he is ridden badly, if his mouth is treated roughly or if he is galloped about and 'hotted-up' he will soon start star-gazing and then the muscles in the lower half of his neck will develop. Gradually the top of his neck will become weaker and the bottom thicker and stronger until it is quite impossible for him to carry his head correctly.

Ponies in this state are very difficult to control and their stiff backs make them uncomfortable to ride. All their paces, walk, trot, canter and gallop are spoiled and generally they jump far too fast and crash their fences with their forelegs.

It takes a long time and much patience to re-school a bad star-gazer. He must wear a thick snaffle or a vulcanite pelham with a loose curb-chain as these are mild bits, and he must be walked round and round a school

A good Riding School has somewhere to give lessons.

Well dressed riders.

A good rider sits up and looks proud.

This rider is sitting correctly, but her hands are too low causing her pony to overbend.

An incorrect seat. This rider has her stirrups too short and is sitting too far back.

Incorrect. This rider has her irons right home instead of under the ball of the foot and her stirrups too short.

A correct seat for ordinary riding.

The canter.

on a loose rein until he learns to lower his head and stretch out his neck. Then the rider, being very gentle with her hands and tactful with her legs, has to teach him to halt without throwing up his head. Once the pony realizes that if he 'accepts the bit' with his head in the correct place his mouth will not be hurt he begins to improve.

But, as unfortunately he forgets this lesson the moment he becomes excited he has to be ridden quietly for several months, until his neck muscles have changed, until the top ones have become powerful and the lower ones diminished, allowing him to carry his head in the correct position naturally and without effort.

### *Martingales*

Helpful people may tell you that the way to deal with a star-gazer is to put him in a martingale, but this is not a cure. A properly adjusted standing martingale will prevent a pony which flings his head about hitting you in the face while you are re-schooling him, but it can't give him a good mouth or a correct head-carriage. Experienced riders use them on unpredictable young horses which may become over-excited; you might, for instance, put on a martingale the first time you took a young and half-schooled pony to see hounds, but they are not allowed in dressage tests and they are never worn in showing classes as they are considered an admission of bad manners.

Show-jumping riders and polo players frequently use

martingales, but as they want their horses for their one particular activity and do not mind if they are unpleasant to ride or difficult to control outside the ring or the polo ground they feel that any short cut to success is justified.

Running martingales, which are attached to the reins instead of the noseband, are not suitable for inexperienced riders as it is all too easy to make a pony overbend in them and there is no point in exchanging one fault for another.

*Ponies which open their mouths*

When a rider on a well-schooled pony feels the reins the pony drops his nose and opens his mouth slightly as he relaxes his jaw and accepts the bit which he may chew or champ a little. Unschooled or spoiled ponies evade the bit instead of accepting it and one way of doing this is to open the mouth wide.

If you have one of these headstrong ponies that charges off with his mouth open, ignoring your aids to turn, slow up or halt, a dropped noseband instead of the ordinary cavesson sort will help to cure him in conjunction with your legs and seat. Drop nosebands are worn lower than the ordinary ones, but they mustn't be worn too low or they press on the pony's nostrils and interfere with his breathing. The front strap of the noseband should be as high as it can be while allowing the back-strap to fit in the chin groove like a curb-chain. A drop noseband should only be worn with a snaffle and it passes outside and below the ring of the bit. When you buckle the back-strap allow room for about three fingers in the chin groove, this will allow the pony to open his mouth a little when he accepts the bit and relaxes his lower jaw. If you prevent him from doing this you will make it impossible for him to develop a good mouth.

*Overbending*

By looking carefully at good riders on well-schooled horses you can get a picture in your mind's eye of how a trained horse should look. But when you see a horse like this going collectedly with an upright carriage, his back short, his hind legs under him, his neck arched, his nose dropped it is important to remember that it would be quite wrong to attempt to make a young or a half-schooled pony go in the same manner.

A young pony should look long and low. The upright collected position only comes about very gradually as schooling develops the pony's muscles and brings his hind legs under his body.

Riders who are in a hurry to make their ponies look schooled sometimes use double bridles, pelhams, or running martingales to bring the pony's nose in and make him arch his neck.

But the pony only looks schooled to people who know very little about riding and his rider has none of the benefits of schooling for the pony's hind legs are trailing along behind him. Generally his stride becomes short, he moves without impulsion and he overbends:

that is he drops his nose too much and brings it too close to his chest, usually by bending in the neck instead of at the poll.

In all collected work the pony's poll - the part of the head between the ears from which the forelock grows - must be the highest part of him. If the neck is higher than the poll the pony is overbending. In this position he is behind the bit; the rider's hands cannot make contact with his mouth.

A quiet pony that overbends will be rather a dreary ride at the slow paces but he may become uncontrollable when asked to gallop or jump because the rider will have to let him extend his head and neck, and, in this position, he will prove quite unschooled. Lively ponies which overbend can be rather alarming to ride as they use their impulsion for going backwards; they are very difficult to jump.

If you have a pony which overbends, ride him in a plain snaffle. Use your legs and seat a lot and try to get him to go with a long outstretched neck instead of an arched one.

If you have a well-schooled pony, don't give him too much slow collected work at a time - let him extend too and at frequent intervals during your schooling let him rest his neck muscles by stretching out his neck as you ride at a walk on a very long rein.

Out hacking, ponies should always be given a certain amount of freedom and allowed to enjoy themselves, the rider who is afraid to go out of a collected canter or who is always holding his pony back will change a well-schooled pony into a constricted, excitable and very likely overbent animal in no time at all.

If you are this sort of rider you will probably find that you are sitting with your legs too far forward and that you have got into the habit of using your hands too much because you are not in a position to use your legs and seat.

### *Bolting*

Real bolting is rare. When a pony bolts he loses his self-control. Generally he has had such a fright that he doesn't know what he is doing. When people tell you that their ponies have bolted with them they usually mean that they couldn't stop. This isn't at all the same thing; if a pony gallops you home to his stable he definitely isn't bolting, he's just refusing to stop.

### *Refusing to stop. Emergency measures*

I have said that the way to deal with a pony which won't stop is by quiet schooling. By improving his balance, by teaching him to carry his head in the correct place and to obey the leg and accept the bit. This is the long-term policy to be carried out on your own pony, it's not much help if you suddenly find yourself out of control, and something has to be done quickly.

If this happens to you in an open space where there is plenty of room around you and not too many people about you can turn the pony in a circle. It may have to be a large one at first, but gradually make it smaller and then keep the pony cantering round it after he is willing to stop. This will quieten him down and also get you riding him forward again. Remember that he will behave worse and worse if you become nervous and start holding him back.

If a pony makes a dash for the exit to the ring at a gymkhana or for the main road when you're cantering across a common, you will have to stop him quickly and on the straight.

If you intended galloping you will have short reins but, if not, shorten them so that your hands are over the withers and you have a strong contact with the pony's mouth. Put one hand down and lock it hard against the withers, move the other hand upwards and backwards and at the same moment sit down in the saddle and use your legs and seat.

You won't improve a pony's mouth or manners if you have to use severe aids like these often, so try to keep out of situations where they are necessary. Don't gallop over commons or near main roads if there is any doubt about your being able to stop. Don't take your pony to a gymkhana until you know that you can control him in company; try him out hacking with friends or at a pony club rally first.

Never expect a gate to stop a pony that is out of control, he may try to jump it at the last minute and land on his nose. Only steer him into a a hedge if it is thick and absolutely unjumpable and never steer him towards the ring ropes at a gymkhana as over-excited ponies have been known to jump into the crowd. Nor are the hind-quarters of other people's ponies a good barricade, you may lame the pony you crash into and you and your pony are very likely to be kicked.

# CHAPTER SIX

# LEARNING TO JUMP

As soon as you are firm in the saddle at the trot and canter you can start learning to jump and, provided you set about it the right way, there is no need to frighten yourself or spoil the pony.

However brave you are don't begin by cantering briskly at a jump of a metre high and hoping for the best; you would probably stay on but you would almost certainly hurt the pony, either by landing with a crash on his back or by pulling him in the mouth.

There is very little fun in jumping a faint-hearted pony which is always refusing and there is no quicker way of making a pony faint-hearted than by hurting him every time he jumps. Aim to have a pony which enjoys jumping as much as you do and accomplish it by considering his feelings.

*Riding over poles or cavaletti work*

Begin with a pole on the ground; a good thick, heavy pole lying in the middle of your school. At intervals during your ordinary schooling turn down the centre and ride over the pole, first at the walk and then, if your pony shows no signs of nervousness, at the trot. Always look straight ahead, never down at the pole, and keep the pony going quietly but with impulsion.

Occasionally one comes across a pony which is afraid of poles and then one must spend several days or even a couple of weeks persuading him to walk over one and rewarding him with pats and kind words and titbits when he does. Don't start kicking and using a lot of whip; forcing him over by making him more afraid of you than of the pole won't have good long-term results.

An unwilling jumper is a very dreary possession and will always let you down on important occasions, so it is worthwhile spending a lot of time to get the pony going confidently and cheerfully at this stage.

If it is impossible to get the pony near the pole without using rough aids ask someone to ride or walk over in front of him, or failing this, dismount and lead him over yourself.

When the pony is completely relaxed walking over one pole add two more with just over a metre between each of them. Exact measurements are difficult to give as they depend on the size of your pony and the length of his stride.

The poles are now arranged for trotting only and you should ride at the rising trot. It is important to settle the pony into a steady rhythm round the school before turning down the centre and riding over the poles. If he is constantly changing his speed or his head-carriage or the length of his stride he will not be able to trot over the poles properly and if you are holding him back he may try to jump them. So practise your trot until it is steady and even and you have the feel that you are riding the pony forward with every stride, never holding him back, and look ahead, never down at the poles.

As the pony becomes used to cavaletti work he will begin to round his back, lengthen his stride and stretch out his neck. This is as it should be and will make him a better jumper by improving his style. You must play your part by keeping with him when he lengthens his stride. If you feel a backward thrust in your chest or find that you are landing in the saddle with a bump, you are being left behind and you should check your leg position, probably you are no longer riding with your stirrup leather perpendicular to the ground.

You must be careful to allow the pony to stretch his neck by following with your hands. This does not mean that you should ride with a loose rein or still less that you should suddenly loosen them on reaching the poles. It means that your hands, not being fixed in any way, are sensitive to the pony's needs and as he stretches his neck they go forward too, keeping contact with his mouth.

If you have got into a bad habit of resting your hands on the withers or the neck, or if you hold them too high or too low, you will not be able to follow him properly; the straight line from the bit through your hand to your elbow is all-important.

Some ponies will trot over one pole but become wildly

excited when confronted with several. They begin to canter and make enormous leaps generally into the middle of the poles scattering them in all directions.

You will usually find that these ponies are stiffening their backs and carrying their heads too high as they come up the centre of the school, so the first thing to do is to get them going in a relaxed trot with their heads fairly low and the rider must make sure he is using his legs and riding forward. A large circle is usually the best way to accomplish this.

When the pony seems established in a relaxed and rather plodding rhythm you again ride at the poles trying to keep him at the same pace by using your legs and not your reins. Sometimes saying: 'trot, trot, trot',' in a loud and soothing voice and in time with his stride will stop him breaking into a canter. Sometimes holding one's weight back to slowing him into a walk just as he reaches the poles will show him what we want.

If none of these ideas work it is best to practise trotting over a single pole until you can find a friend with a sensible pony to give you a lead. You will need to ride right on his tail so choose one that doesn't kick. This almost always settles down the excitable pony for not only does he copy the steady one, but being right on his tail he has no wish to go any faster and at the same time his rider, finding that he is not going to rush off, can relax too and has no temptation to clutch at the reins.

*Cavaletti*

Cavaletti are poles fixed to cross-pieces of wood. Good ones can be used at three heights - on their feet, on their heads and on their sides. They have caused accidents when piled on each other to make jumps and must not be used in this way. At their lowest height cavaletti count as poles on the ground, but they are rather better as their cross-pieces prevent them from rolling if the pony kicks them.

*The jumping and galloping seat*

In order to be balanced, and with your pony, when jumping it is necessary to shorten your stirrups and ride with the forward or jumping seat.

The correct length of stirrup varies from person to person. It depends too on what type of pony you are riding and what sort of saddle you have, but it should certainly be at least two holes shorter than your schooling length.

As a rough guide, if you are sitting in the lowest part of the saddle with your legs hanging naturally the tread of the stirrup iron should come above the sharp pointed knob of your ankle joint.

With a jumping seat you no longer sit upright but incline your shoulders forward a little and have your reins rather shorter than you would for schooling or hacking. The shorter stirrups make the angles of your heels and knees much sharper and this may feel uncomfortable at first, but you will soon become used to it and you must on no account move back in the saddle to relax the angles; you must sit forward and allow your weight to rest on your thighs and knees and stirrups.

When you have become used to the seat at the walk and trot, try out your balance at the trot by standing in your stirrups instead of rising. Don't stand up high with a straight knee, keep your seat very close to the saddle, your knees and stirrups. Don't allow any weight on your hands which should always be kept clear of the pony's withers and never rested on them. It is as important as ever to keep your two straight lines: the stirrup-leather perpendicular to the ground and the unbroken line from the bit to your elbow.

Now, having mastered cavaletti work and acquired a correct seat, you can begin jumping.

Arrange three poles or cavaletti in the centre of your school and just under three metres from the last one put a very small jump - 30 to 40 centimetres high. Trot over the poles as usual and go straight on over the jump.

Don't become excited and begin to kick or steer, just keep the pony going forward, look straight ahead, never down at the jump, and take hold of the mane or neckstrap. If you have done your cavaletti work well he will pop over without the slightest sign of excitement and without any effort on your part. It doesn't matter if he canters the last stride before the jump, just bring him quietly back into a trot afterwards, but he mustn't canter over the poles on the ground as they are arranged to fit in with trotting strides and no pony can canter over them without kicking them in all directions.

When you and the pony both feel confident over this jump, try one without cavaletti in front of it. Approach it in the same way at a steady trot with yourself calm and looking ahead and the pony going quietly but willingly.

Them make four small solid jumps - thick poles crossed are excellent - in the school, not one after the other but two on each diagonal, so that by changing the rein you trot over two of them or by making a figure-of-eight you use all four. Once again it doesn't matter if the pony canters the last stride before the take-off, but he must be back at a steady trot before the next jump. If he shows signs of becoming excited, ride on round the school and don't jump again until he has calmed down; them jump each jump in turn riding round the school several times in between.

If he is going well all you have to do is to use your legs quietly, riding him forward every stride, look ahead and keep as still as possible.

However much you are enjoying yourself, don't go on and on practising over the same jumps for too long, remember that the pony is doing the actual jumping and that he may be becoming tired or bored.

*The jumping seat at the canter*

While you are still jumping from the trot you can begin to practise riding at the jumping canter. This is a faster and freer pace than the school canter and they pony should look longer and lower than one that is being ridden at the collected pace.

The rider is 'in his stirrups' but once again you must on no account stand up with a straight knee, but, by increasing the angles of heel, knee and hip, you become closer to your pony and lower. The rider who becomes taller is riding with a straight knee and his weight will be too far forward, this will make him insecure and liable to shoot over his pony's head at a sudden refusal or if the pony pecks when landing over a drop-fence. Riding with your legs too far back, instead of with your stirrup-leathers perpendicular, can have the same effect. If you have either of these faults, check the lengths of your leathers as you may be riding too long.

It is a common fault to have the reins too short and the hands too far forward when riding with the jumping seat. This not only brings your weight too far forward but makes it impossible for you to give the pony the freedom he needs when jumping large fences. It may seem ridiculous to bother about large fences while you are still jumping 45 centimetres, but if you learn to jump well the size of the fences will not matter to you. You will always be able to jump as high as your mount.

When cantering, you should have your reins long enough for your hands to stay close to the withers, then, when you jump, your hands will be able to move forward one on either side of his neck to give him the freedom he needs. If you ride with the reins so short that your hands are already half-way up his neck you will not be able to give him any more freedom over the jump; he will not be able to stretch out his neck and therefore cannot jump the full height or width of which he is capable.

*Practising the canter*

First practise the jumping canter round the school then push on a little faster and go right round your field, then slow up again and bring the pony back into the school all at the canter, don't let him drop back into a trot. Keep him balanced and going quietly but energetically, this will mean riding him forward using your legs every stride and you will find it quite tiring so stop at intervals and take a rest.

It is very important that the pony should be calm, remember that this is the pace from which you are going to jump and at which you will ride up and down hills when you go across country; you must be sensible and not allow a flat-out gallop. If he tries to tear away, use your reins and legs together to slow him up; or make a large circle; or bring him back to a trot and get him going properly before starting again.

A balanced pony is smooth and light to ride, a pony which is heavy and pulling is unbalanced and he cannot jump properly in this state, therefore you must always take action at once and never ride on, much less put him at a jump, until you have done something about it.

The gallop. The rider has short stirrups and leans forward. His weight is no longer in the saddle but over his knees, thighs and stirrups.

This pony is going forward freely. The rider is handling the double bridle with great care.

A young determined rider jumps  over a small fence.

A good jump but the rider's toes are turned out.

Another good jump but the rider has lost her leg position and has collapsed on the pony's neck.

A good fence made to look solid with the brush underneath.

This rider is jumping well and looking where she wants to go next, but she has lost contact with her pony's mouth.

# CHAPTER SEVEN

# MORE ADVANCED JUMPING

*Jumping from the canter*

When a pony goes well at the canter, jumping becomes very easy and pleasant. You will find yourself approaching your little jumps with the pony straight, looking where he is going and neither pulling nor being sluggish. All you will need to do is to press a little harder with your legs the last three strides before the fence, move your body forward as he takes off and slide your hands forward. Provided that your legs are in the correct place with the stirrup-leathers perpendicular you will find that it is quite easy to keep with the pony and that your body moves forward naturally. In fact, you may feel that you are sitting still, but if the jump is smooth what you have done is to move your body in time with the pony's movements and this has kept your weight still; it has remained over your knees and stirrups through the jump. This makes jumping much easier for the pony. Imagine how you would feel jumping with an unpredictable weight on your back. A weight which sometimes ended up round your neck, sometimes landed with a crash on your back, sometimes lurched forward just as you were about to take off. You will understand then what a worry it can be to be jumped by a bad rider.

Some people approach their fences with tremendous energy; they flap their legs, wave their elbows and brandish whips, they may even make ferocious noises as well. This is all quite unnecessary. It is the pony who does the jumping, and the less noise and movement there is to distract him the easier it will be for him to concentrate on the jump. The rider's job is to get him going well on the flat and then to avoid hindering him.

*The take-off*

Most ponies take off about the height of the jump in front of it. In other words, they start to jump a metre away from a jump that is a metre high. As a rule it is best for a pony to increase his speed slightly as he comes into a fence so you should teach yourself to increase the pressure of your legs for the last three strides before the take-off. But use them quietly, don't become excited and kick. The pony has to look at the bottom of the fence and calculate the take-off, a sudden kick will distract him and may make him take off too early or too late.

Some riders always kick their ponies on the take-off, but why punish the pony with a kick in the ribs when he is doing what you want? Ponies which are used to this treatment seem to get in the habit of jumping rather fast and with a flat back instead of a rounded one; this makes them inclined to knock down fences with their hind legs.

At times when re-schooling a spoiled horse it is necessary to hit him on the take-off, but only a fairly experienced rider can do this at exactly the right moment and to hit a pony at any other moment during the approach to the fence is madness and will probably cause a refusal.

### *Tack for jumping*

It is very much easier to jump on a forward-cut saddle with a knee-roll than on one of the ordinary straight-cut ones. But most beginners have to put up with whatever is provided and, as long as the saddle is not so straight-cut that your knee is on the pony's shoulder when you shorten your stirrups, it will do until you begin to jump large fences.

The best bit for jumping is a snaffle. If you have to ride in a double-bridle or pelham it is a good idea to take off the curb-chain or tie up the curb-rein, as if anything goes wrong you don't want to hurt your pony's mouth more severely than you need.

If you have a pair of rather long reins you may find that when you pull up your stirrups the reins become entangled round your foot. If so, tie a knot in them down by the buckle. This is a good temporary measure, but if the reins belong to you and are always used on that pony it is really better to get them shortened by a saddler.

*Neckstraps*

If you jump correctly you have no need to hold on to anything, but obviously a learner may make mistakes and there are ponies which are particularly difficult to sit because they cat-jump, and nervous ponies which jump much higher than they need. There is also the first jump on a strange pony who may take off earlier than you expect and leave you behind . If there is any danger of hurting the pony's mouth the rider should certainly hold on to the mane or a neck-strap, but at the same time it must be remembered that this isn't the right way to jump, for your hands should be following the pony's head, giving him complete freedom, while maintaining contact with his mouth and they can't be doing that if you're holding on to a neckstrap to keep your balance.

If your pony has a mane this will do very well for learning and emergencies. If he is hogged he should wear a neckstrap when being jumped by a beginner. A martingale neckstrap is better than nothing, but a leather belt or an old stirrup-leather cut short, which can be buckled farther up the pony's neck are really more effective as they help to get the rider forward into the right position over the jump.

A rider who has to hold on grimly over every fence cannot be sitting correctly - he has, almost certainly, a wrong leg position and he should give up trying to jump until he has put this right.

*Whips, sticks and canes*

A rider should always carry a whip as without one it is tempting to start kicking if the pony fails to obey a leg aid. For jumping it is important that it should be a whip and not a stick or cane. It should be light, not too long, and have a round, flat knob on the top and possibly a loop to go round your wrist, though you can always make one of these.

If you have to jump with a stick cut out of the hedge or a cane, always hold them at the extreme end and never allow any part of them to stick up above your thumb, otherwise if the pony does a bad jump, it is possible to jab yourself in the face or give yourself a black eye.

*What may go wrong*

*Running out.* A pony runs out when he carries you past the jump you are trying to go over. It happens to everyone occasionally, for even the best of riders can be taken by surprise, but if it occurs frequently it is a sign of bad riding.

If your pony runs out to the left, stop him as soon as you can and turn him to the right. If you turn him to the left, the way he wants to go, he will feel sure that he has won at least half the battle. Take him back to try the jump again and give him a short run - four metres is plenty for a low fence.

Now you have to make up your mind that whatever happens he is not going to run out to the left again. If he must run out see that he goes to the right; if he refuses it doesn't matter. He probably will refuse because a pony that intends to run out approaches the jump without looking at it and without thinking where he is going to take off, therefore you have to convince him that he isn't going to be allowed to run out before he actually thinks of jumping.

Obviously, you will use your legs and reins to control him, but you can also sit down and use your seat, you can look in the direction in which you are determined to go, not in the one where he is trying to take you, and probably most useful of all, you can use your brain to outwit him.

When you know a pony you soon learn whether he runs out mostly to the right or to the left, and you can often guess that a pony will run out to the left of one jump because some ponies are standing on that side and to the right of the next because it will be towards the stable gate. Think ahead and be ready to forestall him and, as soon as he realizes that you aren't going to let him run out, he will give up trying.

Some people believe that large wings are the answer to running out, but I don't agree with this, except in the very early stages of teaching the horse or rider. After all, jumping itself is easy for the rider, the pony does it all. It is only the approach which is the concern of the rider. He or she has to see that the pony is straight, balanced and going at the right speed for the type of jump.

At shows and in cross-country competitions the riders walk the course but not the horses, so the rider must convey to his mount what is ahead: when to go fast for a spread-fence or slow up for a straight one, when he can cut the corner, when it is essential to go wide and when the easy-looking little fence they're approaching has an enormous coffin on the far side. This sort of riding needs brains and legs and reins and you don't learn to use them if you rely on wings.

*Refusing*. Refusing is stopping dead in front of a jump. There are a great many different reasons why ponies refuse but the most usual one is that they are afraid to jump. They may have been ridden badly and had their mouths or backs damaged, there may be something wrong with their legs. Young horses may refuse when they are throwing splints (bony knobs on the legs), good jumpers because they have a slight strain, not quite bad enough to make them lame, but enough to hurt them jumping. Old ponies which start to refuse may be developing ringbone or navicular or some other disease of the bones of the legs and hoofs.

All horses and ponies will refuse if they have been jumped too much on hard ground, if they are very tired or terribly out of breath, and all but the very brave and well-trained may refuse when they are ridden at a jump over which they have just had a bad fall or banged their legs violently.

Some ponies are afraid of ditches, some of water; some are afraid of every sort of jump because they have been 'over-faced', that is, asked to jump higher than they can.

Ponies that are weak and tired through extreme youth

or old age, or are thin and in poor condition, will refuse because they feel too tired to enjoy jumping.

If you suspect that your pony has anything wrong with his legs or is weak and thin or very old you must stop trying to jump him - send for the vet and ask his advice. If you pony is young, you shouldn't ask him to jump until he is four and nothing high until he is five.

If you think your pony may be refusing because of your riding, go back to practising over poles on the ground and really tiny jumps until you improve and he regains his confidence in you. If he bangs his legs badly or has a fall, put all the jumps lower until he has re-gained confidence in himself.

If there is any particular type of jump of which he seems frightened, make a small one. Dig a tiny ditch, ride him through puddles, turn two planks into a brightly painted wall.

Not all ponies refuse because of fear. A badly trained pony which argues endlessly with its owner on the flat is obviously going on arguing when asked to jump, and it is really a waste of energy trying to make him jump until you have got him going better.

Normal ponies all refuse occasionally. When your pony does it, take him back a short distance - refusing ponies should never be given long runs - use your legs a bit harder and, if you think he is being lazy because the jump is away from home or from other ponies, give him a tap with your whip.

If he still won't jump after two or three attempts, don't become excited and begin to beat and kick, because this won't do any good in the long run even if it gets him over now. Remember that you want your pony to enjoy jumping. If you are riding with other people ask for a lead, another pony in front may encourage yours; if you are alone, the only sensible thing to do is to dismount and lower the jump.

Some ponies are courageous and will jump anything regardless of how their riders feel. Others, less brave, need to feel that their riders are really determined before they have the courage to jump anything difficult. Never put your pony at a jump unless you are sure that you want to jump it. Riding ponies at fences in a half-hearted manner and then punishing them for refusing is sure to make them hate jumping.

There is no need to jump high. You will learn far more by making interesting courses with doubles and trebles than by jumping one or two large fences. When you and your pony have complete confidence in each other, the higher jumps will begin to look quite easy.

*The refusal of the trained horse*. A trained horse or pony sometimes refuses on realizing that he has his stride wrong and that, as he cannot take off in the correct place, he is likely to crash the jump ahead. He should not be punished for this as he had only made a mistake in his calculations and you can tell this sort of refusal from the ordinary one by his eagerness to turn round and go at the fence again.

At shows combination fences often cause refusals because if the horse takes the first part too fast he lands too near the second fence to adjust his stride and take off again. On the other hand, if he takes the first part too slowly, he may not have the impetus to clear the second jump, especially if this is a spread, and that can also cause a refusal. Since it was the rider who walked the course any blame should really rest on her for not giving his horse a clear enough indication of what lay ahead.

The more experienced, intelligent and supple a horse or pony is the more he will do to get himself out of trouble when he comes 'wrong' at a jump. He will take a very long stride or put in a sudden short one. He'll stand back and make an enormous leap or heave himself into the air with a vertical take-off from right underneath the fence. If it's an easy jump he'll scramble over somehow, but if it's a large solid affair and he knows he can't clear it from the incorrect take-off, but will only bang his legs or possibly fall, he cannot really be blamed for saying, "Help! I'm wrong!" and stopping dead.

This is why the first refusal should incur less faults than a knock-down whereas the second refusal is a disobedience - the horse or pony is saying: "I won't," and therefore it is more heavily faulted than either the first or a knock-down.

Your pony will refuse if he is badly presented at a fence. If you ride him round a corner too sharply and suddenly confront him with a jump or if you put him at one when he is half asleep, thinking of other things and so unprepared; without impulsion he will have to refuse simply because he is not in a position to jump.

It is the rider's job to prepare the pony for whatever lies ahead and as you begin to jump larger and more difficult fences it becomes increasingly essential that you should study his point of view and not ask him to perform impossible feats by riding him at jumps in an aimless or reckless manner.

# CHAPTER EIGHT

# FENCES AND COURSES

*Types of jumps*

Jumps for inexperienced ponies should always be made to look as attractive and encouraging as possible, and if riders and owners want bold free-going ponies which jump with pleasure they must learn how to build the right sort of fences and courses.

Unexpectedly, perhaps, it is solid fierce-looking fences which produce good, keen jumpers. Flimsy jumps are difficult for the novice and make the experienced pony careless as he soon learns that they break or fall at a touch. The rider then becomes over cautious and begins to jump slowly, holding back all the time instead of riding forward. As a result of this the pony carries his head too high, stiffens and flattens his back instead of rounding it; in fact, everything goes wrong.

*Poles*

Poles should always be heavy and thick and not less

than three metres long. It is madness to jump over bean-sticks or two-by-two and though narrow jumps make a good test for the trained pony they are not so good for the inexperienced, whose rider may be tempted to use too much hand to keep him straight. At this stage, remember, boldness is the virtue we want to encourage.

*Supports*

Supports for jumps should be solidly based so that they don't collapse at every gust of wind, but most of them should be movable for the pony learns nothing from perpetually jumping the same jump in the same place and also the approach and landing soon becomes cut up.

Small oil-drums, which can be used standing up straight or lying on their sides, make useful supports for pony-sized jumps. They look less hideous if they are painted.

*Spread fences*

The best jumps to begin your training over are spread fences - triples, doubles and hog's backs. This is partly because the lower rails in front of the high one help the pony to find the correct take-off point and partly because jumping width will give him a good style as well as teaching both of you to jump higher without frightening either of you with a high jump.

You can use cavaletti or oil-drums and poles to make

little spread fences but build them carefully, making sure that you are helping the pony to find the correct take-off and not confusing him. Remember that he would take off not less than the height of the jump in front of it. (Good jumpers and larger ponies make take-offs rather farther away from small jumps). So, if you build a triple, the top rail of which is 60 cm high, the lower rails must be so arranged that they cause the pony to take off 60 cm away, put the middle rail 30 cm high and 30 cm from the first rail, while the third pole can lie on the ground 30 cm from the middle one.

For a hog's back you would leave your highest pole at 60 cm but arrange the other two poles, one on either side of it, both at 30 cm. You can see that this jump doesn't give the pony quite so much help with finding his take-off as a triple.

Parallel bars are more difficult to jump than the other spread fences because the two rails are of the same height and give the pony no help at all; in fact, they are actually a straight fence made more difficult by having width as well. Treat them as straight fences.

*Straight fences made of poles*

Jumps should never have a lot of daylight under them. A single pole, which has been raised to the top of its supporting posts, is an extremely difficult jump since the pony looks at the bottom of the jump to judge his take-off and this one has no bottom. Adding a second rail makes it easier; adding a third and fourth rail will make it easier still, and if a pole is put on the ground a little in front of the jump this will make the pony 'stand back' a bit more.

There are other ways of filling up the gap beneath a pole. Sacks stuffed with straw have a good solid appearance; straw bales themselves are a good gap-filler for the larger or more experienced pony. Bundles of pea-sticks, a row of oil-drums, a log, anything which *looks* solid will do, it doesn't actually have to *be* solid as it is protected by the pole above. If you bring the gap-filler forward a little in front of the pole you will discourage the pony from taking-off too near which is the common fault of all horses and ponies when jumping straight fences.

### *Other straight fences*

Walls and gates have a habit of casting terror into the hearts of small ponies, chiefly because they are only made in large sizes and cannot be put low enough to be encouraging the first time the pony meets them. As the hearts of inexperienced riders are often in the same state the result is a firm refusal even though the jump may be within the pony's height range.

The way to avoid trouble is to make yourself miniatures. It is easy enough to paint bricks or stonework on planks and it's not very difficult to make a three-barred gate. Probably your carpentry will produce rather flimsy fences, but this won't matter as you can jump them with a pole or even two above.

If anyone offers to make you a proper brush-fence ask for it to be low, especially the frame-work which holds the brush, for you can jump it with poles above or you can refill it with taller brush when you and your pony are capable of jumping higher.

The great thing is to avoid battling with a pony who is frightened by being asked to jump a new obstacle at a height that is an effort for him. Until he is fully trained any new fence must be of a size that he can jump with ease.

Stiles are not good jumps for training purposes. They are too narrow and they fall too easily. Ponies are careless over them as a rule and riders tend to use too much hand which causes the pony to flatten his back and knock down the jump with his hind legs.

Road Closed and dragon's teeth jumps are bad schooling fences if there is a lot of daylight under them. Add extra rails. Two poles criss-crossed or, if you can only spare one, place it diagonally, one end on the support the other on the ground; if you bring the ground end of the pole forward a little it will help the pony to find his take-off and the same applies to the ground ends of the crossed poles.

*False ground lines*

As I have already explained, any jump which rises gradually away from the pony is easier than an absolutely straight one. Therefore, if you ever have to lower a fence like a gate by leaning it make sure than you lean it away from him. A sloping jump which has the highest part nearest to the approaching pony is said to have a false ground line. No young or inexperienced pony should be asked to jump a fence with a false ground line. Gates leaning towards the approach are particularly dangerous and can give the pony a fall which may put him off jumping for some time.

### *Natural fences*

Natural fences are the type you might expect to meet when riding about the countryside and not the painted objects of the show-ring. Brushes, rustic gates and rails, which are made of unpainted wood with the bark left on, all count as natural fences. So do streams, ditches, hedges and banks.

If you have your own schooling paddock it is a good idea to dig a small ditch. It can be very small at first. Dig it the full length, about as long as a jump pole, but leave it narrow and shallow so that the pony can walk up and step over easily. Then, gradually, week by week, dig it deeper and wider. When the pony thinks nothing of popping over the ditch alone you can jump it with a pole over the middle or with a brush-fence in front or behind. You can also include it in combination fences.

The paddock hedge, or the slip rains, in the corner may seem a very tempting natural fence as you progress but don't use them as schooling fences and then expect them to keep your pony in; if he is intelligent he'll be over the hedge and in search of company or better grass whenever he feels bored.

*Extraordinary jumps*

A trained pony should jump anything of a reasonable size at which his rider puts him no matter whether he has seen a jump like it before or not. But to reach this stage he has to be a good jumper with confidence in himself and his rider and he has to have jumped a great many different fences; not spent his time going over the same old pole.

If you don't possess a large number of jumps you must devise extraordinary ones to give him the experience he needs.

Coats and macintoshes hanging on a pole usually horrify ponies at first, let him look at them and keep the jump low until he feels confident. Curtains, blankets and horse-rugs can also be hung over poles, wellies or plastic buckets can be stood below. Water-troughs and chicken-coops make interesting jumps for the slightly more experienced pony, but as they cannot be made lower it is no use attempting them too soon and risking a refusal.

You will probably be able to think of any number of extraordinary objects with which to embellish your jumps, but don't use anything which could hurt the pony if he made a mistake and became entangled in it or anything of value to your family which could be crushed by a falling pole or split by a careless hoof.

## *Combination fences*

A combination is a group of two or three fences with only short distances between them. In show-jumping they are designed as a particular test and each combination counts as one fence though there may be three jumps in it. A treble consists of three fences and a double of two.

All combinations test the balance and suppleness of a pony and besides this you can build them to test his obedience or his impulsion.

Inexperienced ponies cannot be expected to display the split-second obedience of the trained jumper as this needs a great deal of schooling and the development of powerful muscles, but they can go forward with energy or impulsion so you build your combinations to demand this. To do this you arrange your fences so that the wider ones which need the greater speed are always at the end of the group.

In a double, you can use two straight fences, or a straight fence followed by a spread. In a treble, you can have two straight fences followed by a spread or one straight fence followed by two spreads, the second spread to be the wider if one is wider than the other.

Besides the order of the jumps there is the distance between them to consider. At this stage of the pony's schooling the distance between the second and third fences should either be the same or longer than the distance between the first and second jumps. If it were shorter the pony would have to be checked suddenly when he landed over the second fence and neither he nor his rider are ready for this yet.

Ponies are such different sizes and take such different lengths of stride that it is impossible to lay down exact distances. At the canter begin by trying six metres between the first two jumps and nine metres between the second and third, then see how many strides he takes between landing after one jump and taking off for the next. A friend can be useful here if you are busy concentrating on the actual jumping. When you have discovered how many strides he takes, you can move the jumps to allow him to take one between the first two and two strides between the second and third. When you have worked out what measurements fit your pony's stride, use them. Later on he will have to learn to jump combinations with awkward distances, but at first we want to make things as easy as possible for him.

When working out the distances between jumps, you measure to the centre of the spread fences.

*Grids*

One of the most amusing forms of combination for small ponies is a grid. It is a good gymnastic exercise and, like other combinations, teaches him to judge distances as well as developing his muscles.

Either cavaletti or poles on oil-drums, 45 to 60 cm high, are arranged at three metre intervals. Begin with three and work up to six.

You must jump a grid at a canter. If you let the pony

trot over he will bang his legs and knock the jumps down, so get him cantering well and with impulsion before you ride at it.

All he has to do is to bounce his way up the grid, he may make one or two mistakes at first but he will quickly get the idea.

All you have to do is to fix your eyes on the centre of the last pole or on something beyond it. If you look at any of the earlier poles the pony will probably run out. Keep still. Don't kick or steer; simply keep him straight, in a canter, and look ahead.

Most ponies enjoy jumping grids, but some excitable ponies enjoy it too much and become wild. Other combinations are good for ponies which rush their fences because the extra difficulties make them sober up and think, but in a grid the jumps and the distances are all the same and so, once they have learned how to do it, they begin to rush and jump recklessly and it does this type of pony no good to grid-jump too often.

The jumps in a grid should not be over 60 cm and they should all be the same height.

*Course building*

As well as giving your pony a good variety of jumps it is important to change the order and direction in which they are jumped by moving them fairly frequently. This also prevents the ground from being cut up and the 'going' becoming deep or slippery.

Once the pair of you can do a good round over a particular course you will not learn a great deal more from continuing to jump it and your pony will either become bored and careless or silly and reckless. Only the timid pony enjoys jumping the same course week after week and he ought to be getting over his timidity by meeting some new arrangements of jumps.

If you can, go to the paddock and reorganize your course before you ride as dragging poles about while holding the pony in the other hand takes twice as long and sometimes ends in broken reins.

The only people who can't course-build in advance are those who share their jumping paddock with cows, since they invariably investigate any changes and knock down all the jumps while doing so.

One of the important points to remember when course-building for young or inexperienced ponies is that you are out to encourage smoothness. You want him to keep the quiet, steady rhythm of his canter all the way round, only accelerating as he comes into his fences, so all the corners and turns must be wide enough to allow for this. If you make sharp turns you will find that you have to check him sharply and to do that at this stage of his schooling you will use too much hand, this in turn will make him lose his impulsion, or, if he is a lively pony, flatten his back. The schooled pony can learn to cut corners, take jumps on the slant and check suddenly, but if you attempt these things too soon you undo your basic training.

For the pony who doesn't enjoy jumping the course should be made very simple and easy. The more difficult jumps should be taken towards the gate or stable and combinations should be kept very low.

But for a pony which is inclined to be reckless and rush, a complicated course with plenty of turns is needed. The turns must not be sharp, so if your paddock is small you may find that you have to circle in between jumps in order to come at the next one properly; this is good for over-excitable ponies. The great thing with them is to avoid having several jumps in a straight line, unless they are in a combination, and don't make your combinations too easy; reckless ponies must be made to think.

You can arrange to jump some of the fences in your course twice and it is more interesting if you can jump them in the opposite direction the second time, but make sure that poles have the sort of supports which will let them fall if they are hit hard from either direction and that you are not giving the pony a false ground line. Triples can, obviously, only be jumped one way, but a hog's back is a two-way fence, so are brush-fences, upright gates and most walls. At this stage of your training the only combination which can be jumped both ways is one consisting of straight fences.

## CHAPTER NINE

## YOUR OWN MASTER

Whether you have been taught to ride by parents or friends, or a riding-school, the day is sure to come when you find that you are your own master and the master or mistress of a pony, your own, hired, borrowed or one that you have been asked to exercise.

With no one to organize you , it will become necessary to organize yourself; a certain amount of planning is essential, for you have not only to fit grooming and riding into your day but the pony's meals as well.

Ponies must not be asked to do fast work on full stomachs as a really full stomach prevents their lungs from functioning properly, and if you gallop and jump your pony when he has just finished a large meal or is full of grass you can cause a condition of the lungs called broken-wind which is incurable and will make him incapable of fast work for the rest of his life.

Schooling at the walk and trot isn't fast work, but a full pony is likely to be sluggish and sleepy, like humans after a large Sunday lunch, and in this state he won't learn quickly or be a very interesting ride.

In the summer, greedy ponies should be brought in or tied up an hour or, better still, two hours before they are to be ridden as this will prevent them from being bloated with grass.

In the winter a pony should finish his feed an hour before you want to ride him. If you intend hacking-on quietly to a Pony Club rally it won't matter if the pony nibbles at his hay-net while you groom him, but give him his feed early and let him eat it in peace while you are having your breakfast. Very few ponies like being groomed when they are eating hard feeds - that is pony cubes, sugar beet, coarse mixes etc that you give your pony in a bucket - and many of them are inclined to be bad-tempered and kick. This is not viciousness but normal horse behaviour.

*Routine*

Most ponies love a regular routine. They like their meals at precisely the same time each day and they are inclined to nag, banging their stable doors and whinnying indignantly if you are five minutes late.

You probably hate routine, but, before you refuse to submit to it, you must consider the pony's views on the matter.

In the summer, provided he has plenty of grass and water, a companion, and either trees or a shed for shelter, he will be able to organize his own life and he won't feel that he needs you. (Though, if he is the greedy, overeating type, you will find that you have to do quite a lot about him.)

But in the winter instead of having a huge moor to roam over in search of food, as he would in his natural state, he is either in a stable or in a bare paddock with no grass left to eat. Naturally, he begins to wonder when his next meal is coming. If you feed him at reasonably regular times he will soon learn to trust you and he will feel quite sure that you are going to appear.

If you are unreliable and vary his feeding times tremendously or possibly even forget to feed him, he won't be able to trust you and he will begin to worry just as you might in the same situation. Worry is bad for animals, it makes them irritable, unhappy and nervous as it does humans.

### *A day off*

Don't be greedy and work your pony too hard. He gets tired and his legs ache and though he may lead a lazy life in the term-time he still needs one day off each week in the holidays.

If he has spent the day hunting or at a gymkhana or even at a long and energetic Pony Club rally let him rest the next day, this will allow him to catch up on his eating as well as resting his legs and his mind.

Sometimes you will find that a day off for the pony means missing an interesting event. Perhaps there is a Pony Club rally the day after a gymkhana , or two gymkhanas running. If they are going to be long tiring all day affairs you must just decide which one offers most and give up the other one. Putting the pony before yourself like this sounds virtuous, but actually it is sound common sense and really in your interest for there is no more likely way of laming a pony than giving him strenuous and exhausting work two days running. The slight strain which would have righted itself with a rest, becomes a sprain when you gallop or jump and you find yourself leading home a lame pony, you spend the next week poulticing or hose-piping his leg and you may not be able to ride him for the next three months.

*Schooling or hacking*

A pony should really be schooled and hacked about equally. If you only hack, neither of you will improve beyond a mediocre stage of riding or training. You will stay a passive rider and not become an active one; he will remain as he is and not develop any of the talent he possesses.

On the other hand, if you always school and never hack, he is likely to become bored and stale - he needs a change of scene and a gallop across country - and you may become stiff and too intent on small things and lose your ability to ride forward and to enjoy yourself in the saddle.

Since schooling demands better weather conditions than hacking, it is probably sensible to school more than you hack when the weather and going are good and to hack more at other times when the weather and the state of the ground are against you.

Wet ground isn't good for schooling. You cut up the field and the pony is inclined to slip when going round corners and jumping. In competitions and out hunting you have to jump on slippery ground, but there is no point in schooling on it if it can be avoided.

Frosted ground is worse and races are cancelled in hard weather as the jar of landing on the frozen ground would lame the horses. You can hack on frozen ground if you treat it as roadwork and ride only at the walk and trot, but you have to be careful when riding through muddy gateways which have been poached by the hoofs of horses and cattle and if you have to cross a sheet of ice, dismount and lead your pony.

Don't school in the heat of a summer's day as your pony is sure to be dull and inattentive. School in the early morning or in the evening: if you want to ride in the middle of the day, go for a hack in the woods.

Don't jump or gallop more than you need on hard sun-baked ground. In a dry summer, move your fences to the shadier and softer corners of your paddock, canter on leafy tracks in woods, on the springy turf of commons and on water-meadows. Save your pony's legs all you can or he may go lame as many show-jumpers do in a hot summer.

*In the school*

Don't school for too long at a time. When you are on your own an hour, counting jumping, will probably be enough for you and the pony. Young, old or unfit ponies should be given rests during schooling and all ponies should be allowed to relax at intervals by walking on a long rein with their necks stretched out.

You may find that you need rests too, especially after a spell at the sitting trot, and it is very much better for you and the pony to stop and rest when either of you is tired than to go on and on doing the exercise less and less well. Don't rest yourself by riding badly, sitting anyhow and letting the pony slop along, stand still or dismount.

*Don't make him giddy*

Don't circle round for too long on the same rein. Change your direction by riding across the middle of the circle and turning the other way or by riding a figure-of-eight and making a second circle in the other half of your school. Always make certain that the pony changes the bend of his neck and body when you do this.

When riding round the school, try to keep track of how long you spend on each rein. If your pony goes equally well on both reins, spend approximately equal time on them; if he is stiff and more difficult on one rein, spend rather more time going in that direction.

Divide your cantering time equally between the two leading legs and rise to the trot on both diagonals; this should also be done out hacking.

*Praise and anger*

Ponies, like everyone else, are much happier if they feel that they are successful, loved and appreciated.

If they get the idea that they are bad at everything and that their owners are fed up with them they become miserable, bad-tempered and unco-operative, again, just like people.

When you are schooling, make sure that you give yourself plenty of opportunities to pat and praise your pony. Don't take the movements he's good at for granted and practise those he finds difficult until he is going with his ears back and his tail swishing.

When you have ridden round a few times at the walk-and-trot to loosen him up, begin your schooling with something he's good at - this will put you in harmony with him.

When you practise something he's bad at, ask for very little: one step of the turn on the forehand, a tiny bend to the left on the circle. It is all a matter of attitude, you can arrange things so that you are either praising him for one step or quarrelling with him over half a turn, and approval is the much more profitable attitude.

Teach yourself to notice a very slight improvement and try to end your schooling with something that the pony can do well; this will enable you to take him in feeling pleased with himself.

When your pony appears stupid and obstinate don't immediately become angry; stop and think. You are the senior partner, the clever one with brains; you are supposed to sort out difficulties. Have you explained properly? Are you asking him to do something that is too difficult for his stage of schooling; or his present muscular development? Is he being nappy, or has he lost confidence in himself or in you?

Some ponies are very slow to learn new aids, you may have to think how you can make what you want more obvious and sometimes you may find you can explain better dismounted. It may be that another pony could show him what you want, there is no doubt that they learn a lot from watching each other and that an older pony is a great comfort and guide to a young one.

Check up on your seat and hands. Sometimes riders are so intent on persuading their ponies to carry out a movement that they twist themselves into extraordinary positions which actually prevent the pony from doing what they want. This is common in the turn on the forehand, when trying to canter on a certain leg and is also done by people who look anxiously down or back at fences when jumping, by moving their weight they make the pony drop his hind legs and hit the fence - the very thing they were so anxious to avoid.

If, in spite of thinking, you find yourself becoming angry or flustered each time you attempt a particular movement give up trying to do it until you can get help or advice from a more experienced rider.

*Don't over-jump*

If jumping is your favourite branch of riding, you must

control yourself and not over-jump your pony.

Poles on the ground and really tiny jumps which are no effort for the pony can be ridden over a great many times. But the higher the jump is and the more effort for the pony the less often it should be jumped.

If you make a habit of jumping until your pony is bored stiff and tired out, he may turn into a confirmed refuser.

If you have practised over various jumps during your schooling on the flat and you then jump your course and the pony makes a clear round in good style it is good policy to dismount, pat him and take him in. Later on, when you begin to think of riding in shows and gymkhanas, you will want to raise the whole course and go round again as though for a jump-off. When you want to do this, don't school over a great many other fences first. Loosen him up, get him going well on the circle and over poles on the ground and then have a practice jump as you would at a show. Jump a straight fence twice and a spread-fence twice, then go over your course. If he jumps it clear, put the fences up for the jump-off and if he jumps that clear make a tremendous fuss of him, jump off and take him in. If he makes a mistake over one fence, just put him over that fence again.

Don't go on and on raising jumps. Nothing is more disheartening for a pony than being asked for greater and greater efforts each time he does well.

Never put your pony at a strange new jump when you know that it is nearly lunch-time and that you really ought to take him in. If you do, you will ride badly and he is likely to refuse. Any new or difficult fence should be attempted about three-quarters of the way through your schooling time; you want to end on a successful note, not with a quarrel.

*Hacking*

Going out for rides alone is not like doing anything else alone as you have the pony for a companion. Ponies hate doing things by themselves so when you take your pony out provide some companionship by talking to him at intervals and giving him an occasional pat.

Hacking is one of the best ways to get to know the countryside in the district where you live and if you acquire a map you will be able to explore and find new rides.

Bridle-paths are public paths, but they often lead across private land, so you must be careful to stay on the path and avoid doing anything which could harm the farmer's livestock or crops.

*Gates*

Shut all gates. If you found a gate tied up with three pieces of string, tie it up like that again when you are through. It is obvious that if animals get out on the road they may be run over, but a safe-looking heath or wood can be just as disastrous as they may eat yew and die.

*Crops*

If for any reason you have to cross a sown field, a hayfield or any other growing crop, always go carefully round the edge or headland. If you are not sure whether there is anything growing or not go round the edge, don't risk expensive damage.

*Cows and sheep*

Never canter or gallop through cows and sheep. If there are any on a bridle-path, pull up and walk through them; never frighten or excite them in any way. Apart from the damage they do to themselves - they have a silly habit of charging into wire fences when upset - they may be in-calf or lamb and you don't want to be the cause of a dead baby animal.

*Other people*

Don't gallop past people walking on a path. Always slow right up and give them plenty of room. They may not be used to ponies and anyway, if you go by fast you will probably kick mud all over them.

Because of the traditions of knights and cavaliers horsemen and women are expected to be polite, politer than walkers. In the country it is usual to say good morning or afternoon or evening to the other country people you meet in lanes and woods and fields and especially to farmers and farm-workers near bridle-paths.

*On the roads*

When riding on the road, always shout 'Thank you' or wave your thanks to motorists who slow down for you. Your pony may be perfect in traffic, but think of less fortunate owners and of people riding young horses. If you look pleased and grateful, you'll encourage drivers to slow down, if you ignore them they'll give up bothering. The drivers of lorries, large vans and double-decker buses need special encouragement as if they drive past a young horse or pony at speed they frighten him nearly out of his wits.

A rider is expected to keep in at the side, give signals and know the Highway Code just as a cyclist is.

*A bad habit*

Don't let your pony get into the habit of cantering or galloping in exactly the same spot each time you go for a certain ride, or, for that matter, in cantering every time you come on grass.

If there are not a great many good places for a canter in the district where you live you may feel that as soon as you arrive at one of them you must set off at once. After a few times the pony will begin to feel this, too, and before long he'll be setting off whether you want him to or not, especially if the canter is towards home. It is bad horsemanship to allow this to happen.

Of course you can't do without your canter, but whenever you are not pressed for time, trot across the field in the usual direction, then turn and canter back and finally walk or trot across again. By doing this you will have a pony which waits to see what you plan next instead of one that tries to seize the initiative and then fights, argues and pulls when you say 'No'.

*Hills*

Going up and down hill is a good exercise for your pony. It will develop his muscles and improve his balance; it will make your seat more secure and give you confidence in each other.

Always check your girths before tackling steep hills; you don't want your saddle to slip.

Riding up hills is easy, lean well forward and give the pony as much rein as he wants. For steep hills, or when going up fast, pull up your stirrups and ride with the jumping seat as this will give you a better feel and you'll enjoy yourself more as well as being lighter for the pony.

Some people are frightened by riding downhill, so begin with a gentle slope and walk down, leaning slightly forward and letting the pony go with a long neck. For steeper hills and riding down at the trot, canter and gallop you need short stirrups and a jumping seat - this will enable you to keep with him and you won't be tempted to lean back or stick your legs forward.

It is very important that you should ride the pony forward when going downhill and not try to hold him back.

If you ride him forward his hind legs will come under him, his head will stay in the correct place and he will be balanced. Don't hang on to the reins. If the pony needs slowing up, use your reins and legs together, in the usual way, and the moment he responds relax the rein-aid.

Don't try trotting down hills until you feel safe and happy riding down at the walk. Practise down little slopes, banks, dips and quarries - it will help to make your pony handy and bold. Don't trot downhill on the roads or on rough stony lanes.

*Water*

When you see a decent-sized puddle ride through it. One day you may want to jump water or jump into a water-splash and the sooner you begin your training the better.

If your pony is afraid of water, begin with tiny puddles which scarcely wet his hoofs and work your way up to larger ones. If he is the sort of pony which tries to lie down in water, get him going with impulsion and ride him through at a brisk trot.

*Young ponies*

Young ponies shouldn't be ridden alone on the roads by any but very experienced riders. If ridden by the inexperienced they need an older pony to lead the way past dogs and dustbins and all the other things which horrify them and cause them to shy.

Ponies which are afraid of traffic also need a companion to go outside them or ahead of them when they meet large lorries and high vans.

*Riding with friends*

Ponies are gregarious, which means that in their natural state they live in herds. If you pony has to live alone he may become over-excited and silly when he meets other ponies; the answer is to let him meet them more often not less. But when riding in company you must be careful to keep a length away from the other ponies' heels. A kick can break a leg and though yours can be mended if your pony breaks his he will probably have to be put down. Some unsociable ponies always kick and for no particular reason, but normally good-tempered mares may kick when they are in season, which is about every three weeks during the spring and summer months and ponies , standing in a group while their riders talk, sometimes work up little quarrels and then swing round and begin to kick.

*Jumping with friends*

If your friends are of the unimaginative type they may want to jump for hours on end or dare you to attempt vast heights. You must be firm but tactful. Suggest a competition with the jump-off 'against the clock' - that is, timed. This will produce a winner without too much jumping and people on young or inexperienced ponies need not try to go fast.

Remember that the height you can jump has little to do with your riding ability, it depends on your pony: he may have a talent for jumping high or he may not. All you can do is to train him to jump a small course well and then, by putting up the jumps a little at a time, gradually find the height of which he is capable. If you try to discover this too soon in his training you may turn him into a refuser. Use your judgement. If he is carrying you over with confidence, you can raise them another few centimetres. If he feels uncertain of himself, leave them where they are; if he is refusing, put them down.

*Racing*

Friends who want to race can be a nuisance. If your pony is a staid and sober sort it won't hurt him, provided he is fit and you don't ride too hard, but if he is excitable, already inclined to go faster than you want and the sort who carries his head too high and rushes his fences, you must *not* race him. If you are out hacking, and the others want to race, insist on cantering on ahead and acting as judge. If they all set off at a gallop unexpectedly, don't try to hold an excitable pony back; let him go on with the leaders and concentrate on keeping him balanced and between the hand and leg.

## *Gymkhana events*

If you have a steady pony you can ride him in gymkhana events without doing him any harm. Excitable ponies can practise musical poles (or oil drums) as this has a quietening effect, provided the rider doesn't become too competitive and begin to kick or pull.

Sometimes among a group of friends, there is a younger brother or sister or a young pony who would be better racing at the trot, and as this is just what the excitable pony needs they should be paired off to race against each other.

Friends can be useful. They can give leads to sticky ponies, shout out which leg you're on if you're not sure and help to make courses. But don't be overawed by friends who think they ride well. Judge for yourself.

Pitched battles with bolshy ponies, uncontrolled galloping, hurtling over large single fences are not the signs of a good rider.

It is in being able to walk or gallop as you want, in jumping round a course in good style, in making riding look easy and smooth and in having a happy and willing pony that the first signs of riding well are to be found.

# CHAPTER TEN

# SHOWING

Entering for a showing class at a local or Pony Club show can be an excellent way of introducing the young pony or the novice rider to the ring, but showing a pony seriously requires a great deal of hard work, and those who don't enjoy tack cleaning, grooming, plaiting, the washing of grey ponies and of those with white socks, should take up some other branch of competitive riding. Showing also demands a good deal of coat brushing and boot polishing as you are expected to be as tidy and well-groomed as your pony. Some people have mothers who enjoy doing all this work for them, but such mothers are a rarity; most of them are far too busy.

### *The good-looking pony*

Good conformation, the first essential of a show pony, is not considered good merely for the sake of appearance it is also the shape which makes a pony pleasant to ride. A sloping shoulder is better than a straight one as the saddle is carried further back, the rider has a lot in front of her and the pony will have a longer, smoother stride. A badly proportioned pony with a head too large for his body will not be naturally well-balanced and will be difficult to school. Sickle hocks, straight pasterns, over long cannon bones all suggest a weakness of the legs that could lead to lameness and are therefore considered faults in the showing class. A pony's looks can be tremendously improved by schooling: you can build up weak neck muscles and quarters, you can even help him to acquire that indefinable quality called presence, but you cannot change a big head, a short neck, a long back or a straight shoulder.

*Condition*

A show pony must be in good condition, not hard and fit as for a race, a horse trial or an endurance ride, but round and plump with a shining coat. He should look pampered and pleased with himself.

*Turnout*

Unless he is being shown in a Mountain and Moorland class for Native Breeds, the pony's mane must be plaited and his tail either plaited or pulled. Pulling manes and tails is a job for the expert, don't attempt it yourself, but anyone who is neat handed can learn to plait. The pony's hoofs must be tidily shod, over long feet and risen clenches will lose marks, and a last minute oiling before going into the ring will increase the pampered look.

*Tack*

In showing classes the tack does not need to be strong and durable, or even comfortable for the rider; its sole purpose is to enhance the pony's appearance. The show bridle, either a double bridle or a pelham, is made of narrow leather and can have a coloured browband. The saddle is straight cut to show off the pony's shoulder, never a forward cut jumping saddle. Martingales, an admission of a half schooled pony, are never worn, nor are bandages or boots of any description, which could suggest a fault in the pony's action or be hiding a weakness in his legs.

*Behaviour in the ring*

A show pony is considered fully schooled and is expected to exhibit perfect manners, willingness and obedience. He must be well balanced with a good head carriage and impulsion and be capable of showing more collection than is expected of a pony in a novice dressage test. When in the ring he should appear calm, but interested, and both pony and rider should look as though they are enjoying themselves. As you ride round you must keep clear of the other ponies, but remember that you are giving a solo performance, not schooling in a ride, so you trot and canter at the speed which shows your pony at his best. When you are called in by the steward or judge always walk round and join the line of ponies from behind and then, if you are in the front line, begin working out where, exactly, you will perform your show.

*Giving a show*

Your show will have been practised and perfected at home. It should be short and well defined. Judges soon lose interest in competitors who drift about aimlessly. Have your pony standing at attention and walk out smartly when your number is called. A short trot and then, in front of the judges, canter a circle on either leg, bringing the pony back to a trot stride before starting off on the other leg. Don't attempt flying changes unless your pony has been very well-schooled and is completely reliable; you will lose a lot of points for cantering on the wrong leg. Finally halt right in front of the judges and rein back a few steps, calmly, smoothly and keeping straight, then walk forward immediately, and ride back to your place.

*Unsaddling and leading in hand*

It is a good plan - and at large shows almost essential - to have a parent or friend standing by with a rubber ready to act as groom and to come in to the ring and help if you are asked to unsaddle. Then you hold the pony while they unsaddle and wipe away imaginary saddle marks with the rubber. When called, lead the pony out and stand him at attention in front of the judges. Then lead him away, in the direction they indicate, turn and trot back past them. When leading in hand always turn by pushing the pony away from you, rather than by pulling him towards you, as this will help to keep him balanced. When you rejoin the line, saddle up, remount and await the final verdict. If you are not among the prizewinners try to look cheerful and if you do win a rosette always canter the lap of honour in the correct order; passing those higher placed than yourself is considered very bad manners.

# CHAPTER ELEVEN

# RIDING IN DRESSAGE TESTS

Dressage tests are designed to test the training of the pony rather than to judge his looks and conformation, but of course having good conformation makes a pony easier to school and, conversely, good schooling improves any pony's appearance.

Dressage comes from the French word dresser which means to train and is used to describe schooling in the school as opposed to schooling over fences. So, if you have been training your pony to go correctly in the school you have been doing dressage.

To decide if your pony is ready for a test, ride him round the school and settle him into a steady, but energetic working trot with a good rhythm. Check his head carriage: is his poll the highest point of his neck, is he on the bit - accepting a steady, gentle contact with your hands? Is he straight on straight lines and correctly bent on corners and circles? Is he making the upward transitions - walk to trot and trot to canter - smoothly and willingly and the downward transitions to trot, walk and halt without losing his balance, opening his mouth or throwing up his head?

*Marking out an arena*

If you decide that he is going well enough, acquire a copy of the test for which you intend to enter and mark out an arena. The size for novice and elementary tests is 20 metres by 40, and you should mark the corners with short posts or large stones and place the letters, painted on oil drums, biscuit tins or squares of wood, outside the track. In the centre, level with the two half markers mark X with a blob of white paint on the ground, and D and G in the same way. Ponies which are not accustomed to large letters round the arena may shy at them and a novice pony goggling at a white blob on the ground will lose a lot of marks.

*Learning the test*

The best way to learn the test is in bed. Using your fore finger as a pony make it walk, trot and canter its way round the test sheet arena until you have the words and the movements firmly in your mind and can visualize them easily. You should also practise facing in the opposite direction, for, if you have always imagined and ridden in an arena with C to the north it is very disconcerting to arrive at a competition and find it marked out the other way round, with C at the southern end.

## DIAGRAM OF ARENA

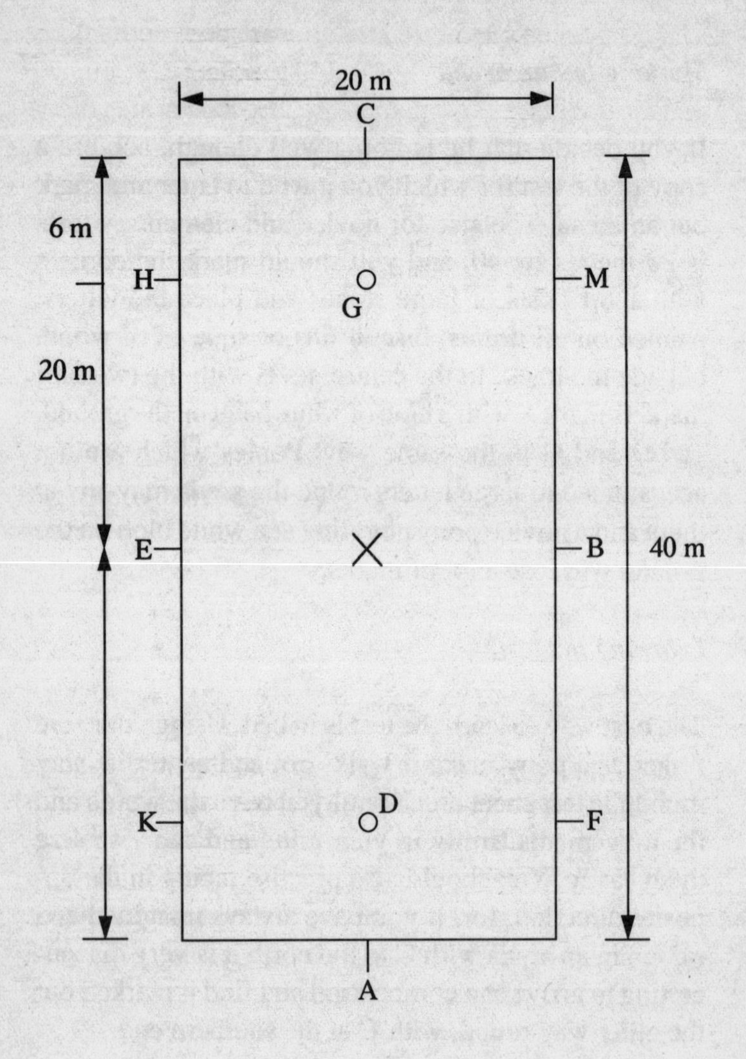

*Practising the test*

Don't ride the whole test too often on your competition pony; if he learns it he will begin to anticipate your aids and this will lose you points. Practise the various movements, but in a different order or with extra circles and walking on the long rein in between. Always begin by entering at A, but then ride round for a bit, do some circling in the arena before turning up the centre and, if the test asks for it, making a halt and bow at X.

If you find it very difficult to remember the test at the same time as riding it, ask a friend to Command you. A Commander shouts out each movement shortly before the rider comes to it, but remember that a clever pony will be learning the test too. So, if you find you need a great deal of practice, dismount and trot and canter through the test on your own feet, or borrow another pony for some of your practising.

*Tenseness*

Many riders, who think nothing of facing huge fences showjumping and cross country, tense up when riding a dressage test, and a tense rider always leads to a tense pony. The Chinese had a saying 'Fear runs down the reins' and this is true of all your feelings, so if you feel yourself tensing up take deep breaths and try to relax your neck and shoulder muscles.

*The halt*

When you ride down the centre of the arena look straight ahead and above the judges rather than at them. If you have to have to halt at X don't look for the marker on the ground, watch one of the half markers out of the corner of your eye and halt level with it.Of course you want your halt to be perfect so you sit down and ride your pony into it, praying that he will halt square. If the halt is a good one make sure the judges see it; take your time over the salute. If the halt is a bad one don't try to improve on it, for immobility is part of the halt and a fidgeting pony will lose even more points. If you make a bad halt when practising, just ride on calmly and try again. Riders who make too much of an issue about halting in the arena find themselves with neurotic ponies which refuse to stand. The secret is to make correct halting a habit, for both you and the pony, even when out hacking with friends.

To salute the judges, a boy puts his reins in one hand and takes off his hat. A girl puts her reins in one hand and with the other straight by her side, bows. Then quietly, and without hurrying the reins are restored to two hands and the rider moves off at the pace demanded.

*Lengthening the stride at the trot*

Once again it is the use of the hindquarters which gives the pony the impulsion and power to extend his stride rather than trot faster and, once again, it is only long patient schooling that will build up his hindquarters and teach him to use them. Some ponies are naturally short striding which makes it difficult for them to show much difference between their working and extended trots, but the rider must do his or her best and, by making the transitions smooth and keeping the pony balanced and energetic, gain as many marks as possible.

*Cantering on the wrong leg*

If your pony leads on the wrong leg, stop and correct him immediately. You will lose marks, but a wrong leg uncorrected will lose you *all* the marks for that movement.

*Circles*

The circles using half the arena may be smaller than those you practised in your school. This shouldn't worry you at the trot, but you may find that at the canter the pony is going too fast and in an unbalanced manner. As this is a sign that his hind legs are not coming far enough under his body the worst thing you can do is to try and hold him back with the reins. Practising transitions from trot to canter and back again will help, provided you use your legs and seat, and leg yielding is a good exercise which also teaches the rider to use his or her hands and legs independently.

*Leg yielding*

Imagine that you are walking a circle at one end of a covered school. There are walls on three sides of you and the fourth side is 'open'. As you come to the open side, you turn your pony's head a little more to the centre of the circle and use your inside leg to turn his quarters out. After three or four strides you change your aids to put the pony back on the circle and give the aids to canter on. Canter half the circle, slow him to a walk as you reach the open side and leg yield again. Do this several times on either rein and then, as it is hard work for the pony as well as you, give him a walk on a long rein. You will need to sit tall and still when doing this exercise, and at first your pony will not make the transition to canter without two or three strides at the trot. If you find you are kicking or throwing your body about, this movement is too advanced for you and your pony, and you should return to schooling at the trot for a few more weeks.

Another useful exercise is to practise making the circle at the canter gradually smaller with your outside rein and leg and then larger again using your inside aids. Don't try to make it too small; remember that you can't force an improvement in a pony's balance, it is only by using all these schooling exercises to develop the muscles of his quarters, that you will eventually bring his hind legs under him.

*Serpentines*

Serpentines test the suppleness of the pony and the rider's ability to change her aids and the pony's bend smoothly and fluently at a given point. Leg yielding will help you with this, but remember that your aids should not be obvious; all movements in dressage must be executed elegantly and easily.

*The counter canter*

This is a movement that requires great tact and a rider capable of using the hands and legs independently. When you asked your pony to make the circle larger you used the inside aids, your inside rein and leg, but as he was cantering and bent to the direction of the circle, there was no danger of him changing the leading leg. When in a test you are asked to make a loop at the counter canter you give the aids for him to move off the track and then gradually return to it without changing his bend or the leading leg. So, if you are going round to the left, your left hand will keep the bend and the leading leg while the right guides him back to the track. The movement and your aids must be smooth, gradual and subtle, especially for the independent type of pony which has grown used to changing legs when needed.

*Riding in an arena with boards*

After schooling in the corner of a field or in a covered school it can be rather claustrophobic to find yourself in an arena fenced by boards, some riders and ponies are so nervous of going outside the boards that they give them a wide berth and, by cutting the corners and riding inside the track, score very low marks. Try to have the occasional school in a competition arena, either at your local riding school or pony club camp. If this is impossible mark out the corners and as much of the sides of your arena as you can with jumping poles, but make sure that the corners are true right angles; if some are obtuse the others will be acute and the pony will find it impossible to get round them.

*Tack*

Check that you are using the correct bridle for the particular test: nosebands as well as bits may be specified, so read the rules carefully. Any ordinary saddle is permitted, but martingales, bandages, brushing boots etc are all forbidden. Blunt spurs are allowed in the more advanced competitions, but riders must not carry a whip.

*Penalties*

Losing your way and forgetting the test are penalized by loss of marks on a rising scale and then elimination. In the present Pony Club test you are eliminated on the fourth error. Use of voice in the arena costs two points.

*Riding in*

Ponies vary so much in temperament that 'riding in' time can be anything from fifteen minutes for a sluggish pony to an hour or more for an excitable one. Only a study of your particular pony will tell you how much loosening up he needs to give his best performance, but generally an idle pony will need a short sharp time with plenty of transitions, while an excitable one needs to get used to his surroundings and then a long spell of steady trotting to settle him down. A stiff pony should be put through his usual suppling exercises, but avoid concentrating on your pony's bad points. It is now too late for improvement, so you should try to enter the arena in a happy mood and praising him for doing something well. Above all remember that your fears and anxieties will run down the reins, so try to keep yourself calm with deep breaths and relaxing exercises.

**ALSO PUBLISHED BY**

**CAVALIER PAPERBACKS :**

**Horse and Dog Stories**

**A Patchwork of Ponies**

**Race Horse Holiday**
**by Josephine Pullein-Thompson**

**The Long Ride Home**
**by Diana Pullein-Thompson**

**Horsehaven**
**I Rode a Winner**
**A Pony In Distress**
**Stolen Ponies**
**The Lost Pony**
**For Want of a Saddle**
**by Christine Pullein-Thompson**

**Hamish - The story of a Shetland Pony**
**by Joanna Cannan**

## RACE HORSE HOLIDAY

## By JOSEPHINE PULLEIN-THOMPSON

`` We waited. The night was full of a thick velvety quiet that wasn't silence. There was just the occassional stamp and scrape from the stable as horses got up or lay down. Time passed very slowly and I began to imagine hunched figures creeping down the shadow by the loose boxes ... I had begun to believe in the horse doper again. I watched and my brain grew numb, groaning for sleep.

Suddenly the noise began! We grabbed our mallets and ran across the yard .."

An exciting mystery develops when Vivien and Jon spend their holidays at a local racing stables.

PRICE: £3.25